THEY STOLE OUR CHOCOLATE FACTORY

THEY STOLE OUR CHOCOLATE FACTORY

Lynn B. Schramek

To order additional copies of this book, contact:
Xlibris Corporation
1-888-7-XLIBRIS
www.Xlibris.com
Orders@Xlibris.com

CONTENTS

PART III

Reclaiming the factory

This book is dedicated to Hans and Renee Schramek, their son
Bradley, and granddaughter, Camilla.

PRELUDE

1993

"The Polish government is selling our chocolate factory," Hans Schramek said.

"But it isn't theirs to sell!" exclaimed his son Bradley.

"I know! The factory has been stolen from our family. That factory belongs to us! No one ever compensated us for it! I am the legal heir to that business. I should have received millions of dollars for it!" Hans exclaimed.

The Germans took over the factory in 1939. After World War II, the communists nationalized the business. According to the 1946 nationalization decree, the Polish government would compensate the family for the factory. In 1993, the supposedly democratic Polish government sold the factory to Jacobs Suchard A.G., a Swiss subsidiary of Philip Morris Companies.

"We can't reclaim the factory until we find documentation validating our claim. We must prove that my father died in 1932 and that our family is the only legal heir to the factory. County records show only that my father was the owner of the factory," Hans told his son.

Now, after more than 50 years, Hans and his cousin Alfred "Aldi" Schramek are ready to reclaim what rightfully belongs to their family.

PART I
Before the War
1920-1939

CHAPTER 1

Hans

Hans was born early in the twentieth century in Cieszyn shortly after his parents' first wedding anniversary. His mother, Camilla, had a very difficult and long delivery. Complications incapacitated her for many months after giving birth. The doctor advised her not to have any more children. If she would, her life and the child's could be endangered.

The family lived like nobles in a brownstone building owned by Hans' father, Bruno. Their home was quite spacious. There was plenty of space for the maid Suzie and nanny Stephie to live with the family.

Bruno rented two apartments in the brownstone to a Polish professor's family and a Jewish wine/spirit wholesaler/manufacturer.

Located in the very southwestern part of Poland, Cieszyn was a small historical and picturesque city. Cieszyn is surrounded by the Beskid Mountains, which is comparable to the Blue Ridge Mountains or the Smokey Mountains. The peaks range from between 600 and 1,200 meters above sea level.

When Hans was very young, he climbed the mountains with his parents. Each Sunday from May through September, their chauffeur would drive them to the foot of the mountain in their Tatra, a Czech car similar to a Ford T. The chauffeur would wait in the car while they hiked. They usually climbed to their favorite peak and rested for a couple hours at a chalet before descending.

Periodically, Hans would get very tired, so his father would carry him until he could continue on his own two feet.

The river Olza, a large mountain stream with trout, divided the city. The eastern part belonged to Poland, which had a population of between 17,000 and 19,000 in the 1930s. The western part belonged to Czechoslovakia with a slightly higher population of 21,000.

Hans, his parents, paternal grandmother and two maternal great aunts lived in the Polish part of Cieszyn, as Polish citizens. Bruno's brother, Wilhelm Schramek, and his family—his wife Cillie and their two sons Rolf and Aldi—lived in the Czech part as Czech citizens.

Two bridges connected the two cities and handled all pedestrian and motorized traffic. Polish custom officials were stationed on the eastern part of the bridges and Czech custom officials stayed on the western part. The traffic on the bridges was usually quite heavy. The citizens of both towns were issued identification papers, which allowed them to cross the bridges at any time.

One day Bruno bought a toy Dachshund for Camilla. It was from a kennel on the Czech side of the bridge. It would have been very cumbersome and costly to bring the dog legally to Poland. It was wintertime. Bruno put the tiny dog in the inner pocket of his heavy fur coat. As he walked across the bridge, Bruno prayed the animal would not make a sound. Even though he knew most of the customs people quite well, such an incident could have caused unnecessary troubles. The little creature was yapping until Hans and his father reached the bridge. Then, like magic, the dog became mute until they got home. Bruno, who was usually a calm person, was a nervous wreck.

Smuggling was common for years. People smuggled petty items, up to real heavy contraband. Some walked across the bridges; others walked across the river Olza through shallow spots. Many things were much less expensive and of better quality in Czechoslovakia than in Poland. Likewise, a few food items, such as smoked meats, were cheaper in Poland.

Many people smuggled fur coats across the bridge. They would wear an old coat across the river and return wearing a newly purchased valuable coat, large diamonds and other precious stones.

Sometimes neighbors would report each other. When this happened, the border police would come search the house. They would tear apart everything and turn it over. If smuggled items were found, a hefty fine was assessed. The border police would confiscate the property and suspend the individual's right to cross the border for a year or two. The local government sold the confiscated items at auctions held twice a year.

CHAPTER 2

Hans' Ancestors

Camilla Bluemel Schramek was born May 13, 1895, in Brno, the second largest city in Czechoslovakia. During the beginning of the 20th century, Brno was very industrial with excellent educational facilities and a rich cultural life for its time.

Her father Leopold was self-educated, yet extremely ambitious. He was hungry for knowledge. He became a very successful businessman. He was the primary manufacturing representative in Czechoslovakia for Matthias Salcher & Sons, a large manufacturer of all types of buttons. He had a store where a few employees sold buttons both wholesale and retail. He became quite wealthy. Camilla enjoyed playing with the button samples mounted on cardboard when she was young.

Camilla's mother Charlotte was an old-fashioned type of woman. She found happiness in marriage and family.

Camilla was hungry for knowledge like her father.

Leopold and Charlotte were very happily married.

Leopold had been previously married. He had three children from his first marriage. Their names were Oscar, Robert and Kathe.

Oscar died young. He was mentally retarded.

Camilla's half-brother Robert was 10 years older than she was. Robert, like his father, was tall by European standards. Camilla loved him, but never understood him. He had a charming personality, but he wasn't honest. For example, Leopold gave Robert money for his college education. Robert was enrolled, but he didn't go.

Kathe, Camilla's half-sister, was also mentally retarded. She was institutionalized when she was young. Camilla visited her occasionally.

Leopold died when Camilla was 15 years old. He had stomach problems. He was in his early fifties.

After his death, Robert took over Leopold's button business, but he didn't do well.

Robert was an atheist. He married a Jewish woman from a poor family. She was a nice person and an excellent wife. Rudy and Robert had two girls—Maria and Ava. Maria had dark, curly hair. Ava had a fair complexion.

Camilla was very gifted musically and studied piano. She became a concert pianist, specializing in classical, romantic music— Beethoven, Chopin, Liszt, Schuman, etc. Many artists and singers like Maria Jeritza, Leo Slezak and Julius Patzak grew up and studied in Brno and had their debut at the well-known Brno State Theatre. Those people became internationally known celebrities and performed all over the world, including the U.S.A.

Camilla took piano lessons from Professor Janoch. After her father Leopold died, she did not have the money to continue her costly piano lessons. When she told the professor, he encouraged her to teach piano lessons.

"Don't worry, my child," Janoch said. "I am constantly getting requests to teach beginners. Since I teach only very advanced students, I refer all the beginners and intermediate students to my wife. She, too, has more students than she can teach. So, if you will allow me, I will launch your teaching career by referring students to you. You will make more than enough money to pay for your future lessons with me."

That proved to be true. By the time Camilla was ready to start her concert career, she had more than 30 students.

Camilla also studied French and earned a state board high school teaching certificate. When Camilla was in school, Czechoslovakia was still ruled by the Austo-Hungarian Empire. German was the primary language spoken in schools. Camilla studied German literature, shorthand, acting, music theory and composition.

Camilla's mother, Charlotte, constantly tried to persuade Camilla to marry. Charlotte discouraged Camilla from what she considered to be excessive studying.

Charlotte went as far as arranging a wedding for Camilla. But Camilla knew that she was not in love and decided not to go through with the plans her mother had made for her. After Camilla constantly threatened to kill herself at the wedding, Charlotte finally gave in and agreed with Camilla's decision not to marry her first fiancé, who was a wealthy shoe manufacturer and close friend of her half-brother Robert.

Charlotte had three sisters—two spinster sisters living in Cieszyn, Mathilde and Agnes, and Paula who was married. They owned a dry goods store. They sold linen and material to peasants, so they could make their own dresses. It was a well-established, profitable business.

Mathilde made good money from the store, but she lived only on the interest. She lived in a small apartment on the third floor of the building housing their store. Mathilde wanted to leave most of her money to her niece Annie, Paula's daughter.

Mathilde and Agnes knew the Schramek family very well. They arranged for Camilla and Bruno Schramek to meet.

Bruno had also recently broken an engagement. His previous fiancée's nickname was Ollie. She was known for her "fish eyes."

Although Camilla was initially against meeting Bruno, she decided to accept her aunts' offer to please her mother.

Charlotte had been diagnosed with leukemia and told she had only a year to live. She desperately wanted Camilla to get married.

"Are you going to grow old as a spinster? Don't you think it's time you find a nice man to marry? I wish you would marry before I die," her mother would say.

Her mother's urgency convinced her to meet Bruno.

Camilla was petite, good looking, smart and likeable.

Bruno was overweight and looked like he was in his mid forties, although he was only 35 years old.

On a very warm spring day, Bruno took a four-hour train ride to Brno to Camilla's home. After climbing the three flights of stairs leading to her apartment, he was dripping with perspiration.

At first, from a physical standpoint, the situation didn't look very promising. However, as they got to know each other better, Camilla discovered that Bruno had a good sense of humor, was a good dancer, good natured, and they were very compatible.

Bruno found Camilla attractive and gifted in many ways. She also had a substantial dowry of 100,000 crowns in cash, corresponding to approximately $100,000 (U.S.) today, which Bruno also found quite attractive.

After a few visits, Camilla went to Cieszyn to meet Bruno's family and to see his brownstone and a new city that was to become her home.

After Bruno promised that Camilla could continue her promising career as a recitalist, accompanist and chamber musician, they became engaged. Her mother's dream came true. They married in September—one year before Charlotte died.

CHAPTER 3

Bracia Schramek TIP TOP

When Hans was very young, his father Bruno and his Uncle Wilhelm conceived the idea to start a business manufacturing Neapolitans, which are small layered sugar wafer bars filled with hazelnut, chocolate, coffee and lemon creams. The two brothers didn't know how to make wafers, so they hired 10 girls and one baker who knew the recipe.

They rented a large room and an adjoining store on the ground floor of a building owned by Bruno's mother, Hermina. They purchased the necessary equipment and manufacturing began.

In 1925, they started the business by making at least 100,000 pounds of wafers a week. They sold these wafers, as well as all kinds of fancy chocolates bought wholesale from different domestic and foreign manufacturers, in their store. Hermina had a coffee bean roasting machine in one of her basement rooms. She roasted beans for people who sold coffee in the area.

Hermina's building contained the wafer manufacturing operation and the adjacent store, two other retail spaces on the ground floor, and three apartments upstairs. All three retail spaces were accessible from the street. She rented the corner retail space and an upstairs apartment to a photographer named Wellner and the third retail space to an Orthodox Jew named Heller who sold hardware. Hermina lived on the second floor, 10 steps up from the ground level.

The wafer business was doing so well that, after a year, they decided to build a manufacturing plant. This dream came true sooner than expected since money was available. They financed the factory mostly from Camilla's dowry, part of Wilhelm's wife's dowry, and some of Bruno's and Wilhelm's savings.

In 1927, they found appropriate ground outside of the city and started building a factory at 15 Liburnia Street in Cieszyn. They bought many new machines capable of producing a wide variety of high quality products at a competitive price.

They named the factory Bracia Schramek TIP TOP, which translates to Brothers Schramek in English.

The factory opened later that same year at its present location. Initially, they hired about 200 people to work in the factory. Production increased from week to week. All of Poland became the sales territory. They hired representatives in each state in Poland to sell merchandise.

Even though the central and eastern parts of Poland presented heavy competition, sales were plentiful thanks to good management and an increased variety of quality merchandise that was priced very competitively.

Bruno and Wilhelm hired a young man as a technical plant superintendent. He was a German national named J. Pietschmann. He had several years of experience in a large similar Czech factory. He ran the operation. He was a talented production manager and an exceptional chef. Speaking the language of his employers, he became friendly with Bruno and Camilla. He and his family joined the Schrameks on their mountain trips and were frequent guests in their home.

CHAPTER 4

Bruno's Mistress

At first Camilla and Bruno seemed to enjoy life together. They frequently went dancing and took the chauffeur-driven car to a nearby town in Czechoslovakia where the first talking movie pictures played in theatres. Fancy coffeehouses offered the best dancing music.

Camilla practiced piano for three or four hours daily to prepare for a possible radio appearance in Katowice. She kept herself busy refurbishing the apartment. Bruno worked 10 hours a day dedicated to making the brothers' newly built factory successful. He spent the majority of time at work or with his family.

The small town atmosphere, the lack of close friends and the weekly family gatherings with Wilhelm's family and Bruno's mother were not exactly what Camilla envisioned for the rest of her life. She became disenchanted with their marriage.

The chief accountant at the factory noticed the marriage's demise. A clever lady in her late thirties, the spinster decided to take advantage of the situation.

She had a birth defect in her hip, causing her to limp noticeably when she walked. This didn't stop her. Being psychologically intuitive, she could tell that Bruno and Camilla were not happily married.

She befriended both of them, gained their confidence and distracted Camilla by introducing her to appealing and flirtatious young men. These men were eager to be in the company of a charming and good-looking woman married to a rich and influential man.

At the same time, the spinster became close to Bruno. Despite her age, handicap and less than attractive appearance, she became Bruno's mistress and lover.

Bruno and Camilla's marriage soured. Family life became terrible. Bruno was never home. He spent every evening with his mistress. Hans hardly saw him at all. When Bruno was home, the evenings were filled with crying and arguing.

The whole Schramek family got involved in trying to save the marriage. Wilhelm and his family met several times at Hermina's home. They begged Bruno to go back to Camilla and leave that woman who was ruining their lives.

"What are you doing? Why don't you leave that spinster? Your family needs you. Why don't you leave that woman and go back to where you belong," Hermina would say.

"You're right," Bruno would agree.

Each time he promised them, things would become normal for about a week. But his mistress seemed to have a power over him. He would soon turn to her again and neglect his family.

Finally, in an intense meeting, his family convinced Bruno to dismiss her from the factory.

After the spinster left the factory, Bruno and Wilhelm hired a new accountant, Emanuel Hirschhorn, who discovered terrible neglect and sloppiness in the books that she had kept. A young, promising man, Hirschhorn was a graduate of the University of Business Administration in Vienna with a major in accounting. He spoke fluent Polish and German.

Even though Bruno's mistress was dismissed from the factory, their relationship continued. It looked as though Bruno and Camilla would get divorced.

Hans was very attached to his mother. He didn't have much in common with his father. Although Bruno had spent such little time with him, Hans feared that Bruno would gain custody of him if his parents separated. Bruno could afford to hire a better attorney and with the help of private investigators possibly could create proof of Camilla's infidelity—which would be a figment of his lawyer's imagination.

CHAPTER 5

1930

In 1930, an economic worldwide depression began to spread rapidly. People were losing their jobs. Conditions were becoming gloomy.

Factory sales began to drop off. Bruno decided to sell his brownstone to generate more cash for the factory. The family moved to a large apartment on the upper level of a two-family villa surrounded by a large park. Bruno spent most of the profit made by the sale of the brownstone to pay for the rent and utilities for the apartment. Only he was impressed with this place. It was very cold in the winter. Bruno spent almost all of his time overseeing the sales and administration of the factory. He was an occasional guest at his own home.

Hans' nanny Stephie cared for him until he became four years old. Hans was very fond of her.

Hans' best friend was Ricky, whose father was a lawyer and a former school chum of Hans' father. Stephie and Ricky's nanny were about the same age. The two girls made arrangements to meet daily in different parks so the kids could play while they gossiped to their hearts' content.

The nannies spoke German and only very poor Polish, so the children did not learn the language of the country where they lived.

In the early 1930s, Stephie left. Hans' parents wanted to hire someone who was fluent in Polish. Camilla hired a kind woman named Annie to go to Italy with Hans and her. Annie had worked at the factory. At Bracia Schramek, her job was to cut the big blocks of wafers into smaller pieces and to wrap them by hand. After the Italy trip, she went back to her previous job. Annie's Polish was atrocious. She was a German national and spoke only German. Hans' parents wanted him to learn Polish.

Then Camilla and Bruno hired Anna, a governess fluent in Polish. Hans could finally learn the language of the land properly and be prepared for school and later business.

When he became school age, Hans studied in public and private schools in Poland. Since his Polish was not very good, his schoolmates and teachers often made fun of him.

Hans remembers being embarrassed trying to learn Polish in school. In the first grade, Hans' teacher told a story about a pigeon in Polish. Hans was beginning to learn Polish, but he didn't understand that word.

When Hans asked his teacher to explain, she thought he was being disrespectful and trying to be funny. She reprimanded him in front of the class.

Hans went home upset that evening and told his mother about the incident.

Camilla marched to school the next day with Hans, explained to the teacher that Hans was trying to learn Polish, and asked her to help. From then on, the teacher was more patient with Hans and helped him keep up with the class.

"May I go to a school where they teach in German?" Hans asked his parents.

"No, son," his father responded. "It is important for you to master the Polish language. One day you will be a co-owner of the factory and will be practically the only one in our family able to converse intelligently in Polish."

No one else in the family spoke good Polish. German was the predominant language between the Jewish and German nationals in Cieszyn until 1932. The Schrameks spoke German at home.

All the elder Schrameks went to school during times when Poland was occupied by Austria and spoke mostly German. They knew very little Polish. Hans' cousins, Rolf and Aldi, graduated in the CSR from a German high school, spoke only German and were enrolled in universities in Vienna and Prague. They had no Polish background.

CHAPTER 6

1932

By 1932, a worldwide depression was apparent. It was difficult for most people to buy bread or a little meat. The factory wasn't doing well.

As economic conditions worsened and Camilla's and Bruno's marriage was falling apart, Bruno contracted gallbladder stones. He suffered from frequent and extremely painful attacks. His screams could be heard a block away from their apartment. The doctor would come give him a morphine injection to alleviate the horrible pain. Since gallbladder removal operations were only in their infancy, they were only done when there was no other alternative.

Initially, his doctor prescribed a bland diet—no red meat, cheese or alcoholic beverages of any kind. Unfortunately, after a few weeks of strict dieting, Bruno would resume eating everything he liked, including many rich foods such as cheese and salami, as well as drinking beer and wine. Another attack would follow making him miserable again.

After suffering with this condition for two years, he could not tolerate it any longer. Bruno was obviously unable to cope with a strict diet for the rest of his life. He often said that he would rather die than live on a strict food diet. This affected his attitude. His condition worsened with jaundice attacks.

One day he had a terrible attack. The doctors decided an operation was his only hope of recovering. There was no surgeon in Cieszyn with experience in gallbladder removal operations.

Arrangements were made with a German doctor experienced in gallbladder removal who operated once a month in a Czech hospital about 20 miles away from Cieszyn. The operation was scheduled for the beginning of December 1932.

A German surgeon operated on him in a Czechoslovakian hospital. The operation seemed to be successful. Unfortunately, a few days later an infection set in and attacked the liver. It was obvious that Bruno would not survive.

Then something terrible happened. Bruno's brother Wilhelm took advantage of Bruno's weakened condition. He brought two of the best lawyers available to the hospital a day before Bruno's death and changed Bruno's will.

Bruno probably didn't know what he was doing. He was practically comatose when he signed. A friend warned Camilla that Wilhelm was going there with his lawyers.

They told her, "Camilla, take a lawyer to the hospital and try to stop him from changing your husband's will. Wilhelm is up to no good."

Unfortunately, she didn't feel well. She had the flu. She didn't realize the seriousness of the situation. Nevertheless, she didn't go.

They brought Bruno home the next day. A few hours later during the night, his family and closest friends assembled. He died seven days after the operation at age 45.

A few days after the funeral, a lawyer read the will in his office. Only then did Camilla realize how Wilhelm's selfish actions would impact her and Hans. Bruno's life insurance policy, which was previously in her name, had been changed. Wilhelm was now the sole beneficiary of the policy, which was worth about a $250,000 (U.S.). Wilhelm was not only the heir of these funds, but he was named Hans' legal guardian and the sole owner and manager of the factory until Hans' became an adult.

The will said that until Hans reached age 21, his uncle was obligated to pay Camilla 800 zloties a month (valued at about $200 U.S. in 1932). This should provide, according to his judgment, enough money so Hans and his mother could have a nice vacation at least once a year. Should Camilla remarry, the monthly payment would stop. When Hans became 21, he would become a 50-50 partner of the factory on the same conditions as his father. In the meantime, Wilhelm would run the factory.

All of Bruno's possessions—expensive jewelry valued in the vicinity of $100,000—were to be deposited in a safe in the municipal court in Cieszyn until Hans reached age 21.

The will created a tremendous division between Hans and his mother—and Wilhelm. Hans lived with his mother, but Wilhelm supposedly had the ultimate say so.

Camilla considered trying to prove that her husband was in a comatose state when he signed the will. Perhaps, then she could at least win back her dowry. Most attorneys advised her not to fight the will. If she decided to fight the will and lost, she would be denied all material assistance from Wilhelm, according to a special paragraph in the will.

For a month or two, Wilhelm would pay the 800 zloties allowance each month. Then he stopped. He said he had financial problems. He only appropriated money for vacations for the first year.

"The factory is growing," he'd say, "and I need every zloty to keep up with the competition."

When Camilla took him to court to collect past-due payments, Wilhelm would pay for awhile.

Hans and Camilla decided to find a smaller apartment. They hated the large villa where they lived. They found an elegant apartment. Camilla refurbished and decorated it beautifully, and they moved in.

Fortunately, Camilla earned enough money from concerts, recitals and radio shows as a concert pianist to support her and Hans.

Hans progressed through elementary and high school in Cieszyn, learning Polish and gaining a general education. He was happy living with his mother. He made a good friend, Emil Klein, during religious sessions at high school. Emil lived in the same neighborhood, so they could spend time together after school.

In the late 1930s, black clouds (Hitler's rise to power in Germany) started to move in.

When Hans heard about the possibility of war, he asked his Uncle Wilhelm to sell the factory so they could emigrate to England. At that time, Wilhelm had indicated that he didn't believe there would be a war. Wilhelm knew that by selling the factory he would lose some money and that was not in his plans. So, consequently, he told Hans to shut up and mind his school business— best not to mix in where his advise was not wanted.

The factory was doing well under Pietschmann's leadership. Pietschmann and Wilhelm didn't get along, however. Wilhelm had a jealous personality and didn't appreciate other people with talent. Pietschmann left Bracia Schramek after Bruno died and started a similar factory on his own.

CHAPTER 7

1938

Wilhelm apparently did suspect trouble on the horizon. Right before the war in 1938, Wilhelm had the foresight to take a trip to Palestine (before it became known as Israel). As a major collector of stamps, he had a collection worth $100,000 at that time. He couldn't take money out of Poland, so he took his stamp collection and enough money for two weeks. He took a train from Poland to Holland and then a boat to Palestine.

When a Polish guard on the train questioned him, he responded that he plays with stamps when he gets bored.

Wilhelm opened an account in Jerusalem and put the stamp collection and personal jewelry in a vault. Then he returned to Poland.

Five days before Hitler declared war, Wilhelm took out 250,000 zloties from the factory's Polish bank accounts, equivalent to $50,000 U.S., record books from the factory, as well as the company car, his belongings, wife and two sons and left Cieszyn. Although he was Hans' legal guardian, he left town without even telling him about the eminent danger and of his decision to leave town.

One day before the war, Camilla called Wilhelm. The maid answered and told her the family had left—leaving their 80-year-old grandmother behind. She chose not to go.

Wilhelm and his family escaped the Germans by going to Krakow, which was the capital of Poland before Warsaw, at the end of August. Hitler declared war on Poland on Sept. 1, 1939. When bombs started falling in Krakow, Wilhelm packed and drove his family to Lwow, which was in eastern Poland.

While in eastern Poland, Wilhelm collected outstanding money from customers who owed the chocolate factory to support his wife and sons.

The money that he owed Camilla for the previous three months of support was never paid.

CHAPTER 8

The factory

In 1939, the Germans invaded Cieszyn. They took over or stole Bracia Schramek's factory TIP TOP. They rehired Pietschmann, who had quit in 1937 because he wasn't getting along with Wilhelm. Pietschmann left the small wafer and cookies factory that he had organized on his own on the Czech side of Cieszyn.

A Nazi, Pietschmann became the German's trustee of the factory. Since he had worked there for several years, he was familiar with the operation and the remaining employees.

At this time, the factory was in full operation with three shifts and 500 employees.

PART II
During the War
1939-1945

CHAPTER 9

Auschwitz

Hitler's overtures began with inflammatory speeches against Jews, communists and the United States. Later, in 1938, he attacked Czechoslovakia and annexed Austria. These actions indicated that he wanted to conquer and occupy all of Europe without any military conflict.

In 1938 Hitler's intervention with Poland seemed to be very friendly. The Czech part of Cieszyn and other towns around this area were annexed to Poland—thanks to Hitler's temporary benevolence toward Poland. Cieszyn became a city of 40,000 inhabitants, the largest it ever was.

In August 1939, Hitler sent his Minister of Foreign Affairs Ribentrop and a delegation to Stalin to negotiate.

The non-aggression pact between Germany and the Soviet Union, which at that time were bitter enemies, allowed him to conquer Poland without the Soviet Union attacking him. The pact placed all Polish territories up to the river Bug under German protection. The Soviet Union infiltrated territories east of the river Bug.

Hitler declared war with Poland at 5 a.m. on Sept. 1, 1939.

At 9 a.m. Cieszyn became Teschen and was infiltrated into the German Reich. By 11 a.m., Hitler was in the city.

Hitler's Special Service (SS) threw Hans and Camilla out of their home. Hans was 19 years old. The Germans took all their possessions.

They took Hans and Camilla to a temporary ghetto in the city of Sosnowiec.

In the ghetto, thousands of people lived within a few blocks. There was a shortage of almost everything. Hans and Camilla were considered newcomers. They were always the last ones to get rations or any privileges. Among the Jews, they were considered the outcasts, because they came from another city and did not speak Yiddish like the locals did. It was rough. They didn't know what was in store for them.

Fortunately, they had a little money stashed away and a couple of gold coins. It was very dangerous, but everybody tried to buy a little extra food. They had to eat something. If the Germans had discovered that they had some valuables with them, they would have killed them on the spot. Occasionally, the ghetto inhabitants could bribe a guard to bring them a pack of cigarettes or something special. They stayed there for about four or five months.

The government that oversaw the ghetto was called the *Judenrat*, which means the elder Jews. This group consisted primarily of professional and religious people who collaborated with the Germans. They did it in good faith. They didn't realize that they were selling out their brothers and sisters. The Germans told them to make lists of the people who should be transported to labor camps so the ghettos wouldn't be so overcrowded. They were told that the people transported to the camps would have much better living conditions. They would have to work, but they would be taken care of. The *Judenrat* first listed people who came from other cities.

Transports were formed. Each transport took about 3,000 to 4,000 people. Fifty or 60 people were shoved into each boxcar. People could hardly breathe. They didn't know where they were going.

Hans and Camilla were on the third transport. They were taken at night. They were ordered to take everything they had and to hurry. The German Special Service guards put them in trucks.

The trucks took them to the railroad station where the boxcars were already waiting. They were shoved into the boxcars by force and heavily guarded. The train transported them to an unknown destination—Auschwitz.

Auschwitz (known as *Os'wiecim* in Polish) was a little city in Poland near Krakau. It had a population of 30,000 to 40,000 people. The Germans built one of the worst concentration camps at Auschwitz. Barbed wire and electric fences surrounded the camp. Those who were deported there were thoroughly secured like prisoners. It was practically impossible to escape.

Under normal conditions, the ride would have taken three or four hours from Sosnowiec. It took them all day to get there in the boxcars. The conditions were terrible. There was hardly any air to breathe, little food and nothing to drink—not even water. People died in the boxcars.

Later, other people from Cieszyn, such as Hermina and her sister Mathilde, were also captured. Mathilde died while they were transporting her to Auschwitz. She was over 80 years old and very fragile. She couldn't tolerate those conditions. Hitler took all of the money that Mathilde had been saving for Annie, and captured Annie.

When Hans and Camilla arrived at Auschwitz they were ordered to line up. First, they divided the women from the men. Then they stripped them of their clothes and their dignity. They put their belongings in a little eave.

They said, "Now you will be washed and deloused."

They were forced to go into showers.

They were assigned numbers and tags. They didn't have numbers tattooed on their arms like others that arrived later. Fortunately, Auschwitz was not an annihilation camp at that point. There were no gas chambers or crematories yet. Hans and Camilla arrived near the end of 1940 and didn't know what was to come a year later.

After their showers, they were given clothes that looked like pajamas and some rubber shoes. They were assigned to barracks where they slept on straw-filled mattresses.

They were fed three meals a day. For breakfast they were given a liquid that resembled weak tea or coffee and one very thin slice of bread. At noon, they were given oatmeal cereal. The evening meal consisted of soup with two little pieces of potato swimming in it.

If they were lucky, they were given a small piece of herring or a tiny sliver of meat. That was considered a treat.

Since Hans was a young man. He was told to report to the *cappo* (head in Italian). The *cappos* were also prisoners. Most of them were not Jews—but gentiles—and were not political prisoners—but criminals. Some were homosexuals. Some were murderers. They were sent there before the Jews to form the supervisory labor body. They were also guarded by the German Special Services, but they had much better living conditions. They were considered the overseers or foremen.

Hans was sent to the *cappo* in charge of landscaping. Hating any kind of gardening, Hans thought this must be some kind of a joke. He didn't know the first thing about landscaping. Nonetheless, he reported to work with his "green thumb." His *cappo* was very decent. He seldom kicked or beat anybody like the SS guards.

Hans knew that his mother was also in Auschwitz, but he didn't know how she was or what she was doing. These thoughts constantly went through his mind and made his life very difficult.

He worked there for a few months. Then one night, all of a sudden, he was woken up by the *cappo* and told to report immediately to the main office. He had no idea what was happening, and he couldn't ask anybody. "In those days, you didn't ask. You just did what you were told," Hans explained.

He reported to the main office and was told that he would be shipped somewhere else to a different camp with some other people. He was told that because he was young and did good work at Auschwitz, he would be sent to a camp that was practically a vacation spot. There he would be trained in different trades, and they would have much better living conditions. He didn't believe it. He didn't want to leave his mother, but there was nothing he could do. There was nowhere to run.

CHAPTER 10

Ebensee

The German Army's Special Service guards took Hans and a few hundred other people to the railroads, and they were again put into boxcars and shipped to an unknown destination. They traveled for three days and three nights.

Then they were put into trucks and shipped to a camp called Ebensee. It was nothing like the Germans promised. It was a labor camp in Austria. The camp was surrounded by a barbed wire fence and small towers for the SS with machine guns.

Hans later learned that the reason he was shipped there was because of Walter Von P., a former friend who went to school with Hans. Now he was a captain in the German Special Service, who did mostly translation services. He knew several languages very well. He was a very gifted fellow. He knew that Auschwitz was to become an annihilation camp. He couldn't set Hans free, but he was able to arrange a transfer. He knew that Ebensee was a labor camp, and Hans would have a much better chance of surviving there.

Hans was again put in barracks. The next day he was working around the camp, doing landscaping and janitorial work.

Camp duty and living conditions were miserable. The food was terrible and was served in very small portions. Food allocations consisted of one-half liter of coffee in the morning, three-quarters of a liter of hot water with potato peelings for lunch, and a small piece of bread for dinner. Hans was weak, but he knew that he had to be strong and act like a mature man. Young, frail teenagers did not survive. The German Special Service wanted men who could work.

After a week, Hans and those imprisoned with him were blind-folded and marched to a truck station. They were put on trucks and shipped blindfolded to a large factory. When they arrived, the blindfolds were removed, and they did factory work, mostly at machines. Hans pressed out different metal parts. It wasn't difficult. Within an hour he learned how to operate the machine. His foreman was a civilian Austrian who was a decent person. He was not a member of the German Special Services or the Nazi party. Being an Austrian of the old school, he hated the Germans and their domination of his fatherland.

Hans was so hungry that he welcomed opportunities to work a 12-hour day in the defense factories. There they would receive some warm cereal or margarine for bread. Whenever he could, his foreman would sneak Hans a small piece of sausage or an apple, which would help to build up his strength.

The main thing was not to lose hope. They tried to build up their strength anyway they could to try to survive. Nobody knew how long this situation was going to last. One needed stamina to survive. The majority perished. Thousands died of hunger, mal-nutrition or being worked to death. Older people gave up and died.

Through the grapevine, they heard that Hitler was progress-ing on all fronts—he had taken France and Belgium and all the Scandinavian countries, except Sweden and Switzerland. These two countries remained neutral, but horrible things were going on throughout Europe. All the Jews were sent to concentration camps. Many of them were shot.

At Ebensee, hundreds of people were dying every day from hunger and communicable diseases—without any medical help. Some were shot, too, because they couldn't get up in the morning. Those who gave up were called *muselmans*. They didn't have the optimism to survive.

Every month or so, a certain amount of new people arrived at Ebensee. They were usually young people who were still fairly strong and could work.

The living conditions became worse as more people came. Less food was given to each person. The work was hard. Hans was forced to work for 10 to 12 hours each day in the factory. A lot of people were getting so weak that they could hardly get up in the morning and report to work. A lot of them got sick. They said they were taking sick people to the hospital, but they never returned. They were probably shot and buried somewhere.

So everyone tried to stay alive and not to get sick—but that was easier said than done.

Unfortunately, Hans got sick. He contracted typhoid fever. If it weren't for a doctor from near Hans' hometown, Hans believes he would have died for sure. Fortunately, the doctor took pity upon Hans.

The physician, who worked in a hospital as an orderly, was from a town about 20 to 30 miles from Cieszyn called Bielsko. He was familiar with the Schramek family and the factory.

He put Hans in a corner of a barrack and brought him food and medications to help fight the infection. He made arrangements with the *cappo* who was responsible for getting the people to work so that the Special Service wouldn't miss Hans. Only the *cappo* and the doctor knew Hans was sick. Hans' co-workers, even if they knew, wouldn't say anything.

Hans was in the corner, nursed by the doctor, for two or three weeks. Finally, he overcame the infection and his temperature went down.

Even though he was terribly weak, he forced himself to return to work before they caught him hiding. They had stopped transporting the prisoners by trucks to work. Hans had to walk an hour to work, work a 12-hour shift and walk back in his weak condition. Hundreds of people were dying like flies. Hans was struggling to survive.

Approximately 20,000 people died at Ebensee. During the closing weeks of the war, the death rate exceeded 350 a day.

CHAPTER 11

Wilhelm

In 1939, Wilhelm and his family were in a small town, called Buczacz.

Right before a two-week war broke out between Germany and Poland in October 1939, high-ranked Polish officers took off their uniforms and fled to Romania.

One day, ex-officers of the Polish army knocked on their door and asked, "Is that your car? Who is the driver? Get dressed and come with us, or we'll shoot."

Wilhelm's son, Rolf, was the only one in the family with a driver's license. He owned a Chevy. The officers ordered Rolf to drive them to the Romanian border. Rolf did as they said and shortly came back to his family.

A week later, other Polish officers came. The officers demanded that Rolf drive them again. This time weeks went by and Rolf didn't return. Then a postcard arrived saying, "I'm in Bucarest (the capital of Romania). Going to Constanza (Romania's largest port on the Black Sea)."

Rolf sold the car in Romania, which wasn't affected by the war, and booked himself on a ship to Palestine, where he survived the war.

When he arrived in Palestine, he retrieved the stamp collection and jewelry that his father had previously secured for him and started a new life for himself.

Rolf's family wasn't as fortunate. Towards the middle of 1940, Wilhelm's family was in the eastern part of Poland that was eventually taken over by the Russians from the Soviet Union. Soviet authorities ordered the KGB to deport all the refugees who came from western to eastern Poland. They made lists of people and addresses of all the refugees in every city. The KGB supervised the refugees.

Wilhelm's family, along with the other refugees, was forced to pack all their belongings. They were gathered together in trucks and the Soviets transported them to boxcars. They packed 50 people to a boxcar and transported them to the Siberian forests to little places that were previously inhabited by prisoners. The refugees were forced to do menial slave labor.

They put about 200,000 Jews and non-Jews in wooden barracks and issued them work clothes.

If it hadn't been for care packages of food from Rolf in Palestine, the family surely would have starved to death.

They were told, "This is going to be your future home. You're going to live here and die here. This is your future. Forget about your past."

When Hitler attacked the Soviet Union, a temporary Polish government formed in London, England. They made a pact with the Soviets to liberate all former refugees from Siberian Labor Camps. The refugees were permitted to go to different parts of the Soviet Union, except the large cities, to resettle and seek work. Many immigrated to warmer climates. Wilhelm's family transferred to Samarkand. They stayed there until 1945 when they were liberated and sent back to Poland.

Shortly after WWII, Wilhelm was diagnosed with prostate cancer and died in 1946.

Wilhelm's widow Cillie, son Aldi, and Aldi's wife returned to Poland. When they returned, they found that after the Germans left, the communists took over Poland and nationalized the factory, like every company that employed more than 50 people per shift.

Since Cillie and Aldi had little interest in the factory, they decided to go to Vienna with the help of a Jewish organization.

Aldi and his wife stayed in Vienna until he finished his medical studies and earned his doctorate. Then they joined Rolf and Cillie in Palestine.

There were practically no Jews left in Cieszyn. The few that survived found ways to leave Poland illegally and found temporary domicile in camps in Austria, Germany and Italy, where they awaited future emigration.

CHAPTER 12

Liberation

Hans was one of the shortest and didn't look like a strong person. But he had enough strength and optimism to stay alive. Once he heard through the grapevine that his mother was also transported from Auschwitz to another camp and apparently was still alive, he felt like he had been given an injection of adrenaline. This gave him another reason to stay alive—to try to make it—to be re-united with his mother.

In the meantime, the misery went on. Hitler was losing the war. It was just a question of time. They were hearing planes flying above the camp. They were hearing about bombs being dropped. Hans knew he had to gather the last ounce of strength to make it.

Finally in 1945, the war was over. The Americans came and liberated them. The inmates murdered some of the German Special Service guards. Some were arrested. The commandant of the Ebensee camp was arrested along with his immediate helpers.

The American and Swiss Red Cross came to the camp to help nurture Hans and the other starving individuals. They were given daily rations of nutritious foods and medical attention.

They were warned not to eat a lot, but rather to eat small portions three or four times a day. If they got greedy and ate heavy or fatty food, they could die. This happened. A few people could not control their appetite. They ate bacon or other fat-filled food and then suffered from horrible cramps a few hours later and died.

When Hans was liberated, he weighed less than 90 pounds. When he looked in the mirror, he did not recognize himself—he looked like a walking skeleton. While recovering at Ebensee, he got some clothes. His hair started to grow. He started to gain weight and strength.

After a few weeks, he felt that he was strong enough to leave Ebensee. He wanted to go to Vienna, the capital of Austria, where many of the concentration camp refugees were congregating. He thought that if his mother survived, she would go to Vienna, too, and hopefully they would meet. He left Ebensee by foot and hitch-hiked to Vienna. He had a document showing that he was a former concentration camp inmate, and he was authorized to go to Vienna. Whenever he saw a military truck or jeep, he asked for a ride. Although each driver took him for less than an hour, he became closer to his destination.

Within a week, he made it to Vienna, which was a terrible sight. It was bombed out. People had nothing to eat. The gentiles were terribly hostile. Hans just wanted to go to the Jewish community to find out what he could do to rebuild his life for the future. Luckily, he met another Jew who directed him to the place where the other former concentration camp prisoners were gathering. It was a former hospital. They were given care, clothes and three meals a day. They were given choices. Hans was still young and could have stayed and studied in Vienna. Since the conditions there were so bad, he didn't want to stay.

After a few weeks, Camilla came.

"I can't describe the feelings, the joy, that we both experienced, to have survived those horrible years—to still be alive and be able to plan a future together," Hans explained. "How our future would shape up we didn't know. We gave ourselves some time to rest and to listen to what other people were saying about what was happening."

How many Jews survived? The news was terrible. They were told that out of three million, only about 100,000 Polish Jews survived.

Hans was sure that his grandmother Hermina didn't make it.

He soon learned that his Uncle Robert (Camilla's half brother) and his family—his wife Rudy and two daughters, Maria and Ava, had been taken to a camp in Czechoslovakia named Teresienstadt and then exported to Auschwitz where they were killed.

Camilla obtained the necessary papers to ride a train across two borders through Czechoslovakia to Poland. Although it was illegal for her to go from Vienna to Poland, she had contacts in high places. Anything was possible with the right connections.

Once they had regained their energy, Camilla ventured to Brno, her hometown, where she had some relatives. She searched for her brother, nieces, aunt and cousins. She found that the Germans had killed her entire family.

She went back to their former home in Cieszyn. All she could find were two paintings. She took the paintings with her. All of Bruno's expensive jewelry, valued at approximately $100,000 (U.S.), had been stolen. Some said the Nazis had stolen the valuables; others said Polish employees in the Treasury of the courthouse had robbed the valuables stored in the safes before they escaped.

She learned that the factory, at that time, was in tact but not operating. The city fathers had delegated two people to watch over the factory. They guarded against vandalism until someone took over the factory and operated it again.

Camilla found a lawyer, a former probate judge, who agreed to represent her and Hans in trying to regain ownership of the factory and the family's personal real estate. He said it would be necessary for Hans to come to Cieszyn, since he is the legal heir of the factory.

"It's imperative for Hans to come sign papers and grant me the power of attorney to represent his legal interest," the attorney said.

Camilla sent a message asking Hans to join her via people traveling from Poland to Vienna.

Hans came as soon as he received the message.

The lawyer didn't know what kind of economy the communists would create. If he could have predicted what was to come, he probably wouldn't have taken the case. Nonetheless, he took the case on a contingency basis.

There was one court hearing. The representative of the association that was supposed to run the factory declared that the association is willing to decline the ownership of the factory in favor of the original owners.

At that point, a man stood up—a communist—and identified himself as a representative of the Polish workers party. He sited a new law forbidding Hans from regaining ownership. The law said that all businesses employing more than 50 workers per shift on Sept. 1, 1939, were subject to nationalization by the newly elected Polish government and could not be returned to their former owners.

Hans and Camilla knew that Bracia Schramek TIP TOP employed more than 500 people in 1939. It was the fifth largest factory in Poland, producing three tons of chocolate wafers and other products each day. A labor union had gained power over the factory.

They learned that in 1943, Pietschmann influenced the German government to change his status from director-trustee of the former Bracia Schramek factory to its legal owner. He paid 100,000 Reichs marks for the factory, and his name was recorded as the owner in the court's record books.

The city fathers assigned a former bookkeeper and engineer to make sure the factory was not vandalized until steps could be taken to operate it again. The administrative organization responsible for all factories belonging to this industry chose a director to hire people and get the factory back in operation.

Hans and Camilla decided to leave Cieszyn, build a new life and try to completely disregard the fact that they had once been wealthy.

In 1945, the communists took over, or stole, the factory. They renamed it Factory OLZA SA, after the river that flows by it. They also took over the Schramek's orchard and built another building on that land, expanding the business.

In 1948, the original factory was nationalized, according to Polish law.

CHAPTER 13

Hagana

They returned to Austria. After a brief stay there, Hans learned about the Hagana, a secret Zionist organization that helped people go to Palestine (before Israel became a state). This organization would cram as many refugees and survivors of the Holocaust as possible onto illegal ships directed toward Palestine. The British, who were then governing Palestine, apprehended many of these ships, and the passengers were deported to camps on the island of Cyprus.

After a lot of unsuccessful petitioning to find a way to get to Italy, Hans met some Americans named Peter and Jimmy in Vienna. They suggested that Hans and Camilla leave Austria and go illegally to Italy. They wanted young, strong people who would go to Italy and then soon go to Palestine.

Peter and Jimmy gave Hans a letter and told him to take it to their friends—alleged leaders of the Hagana in Austria.

To get to Italy, they needed the backing of the Zionist organization supported by the Hagana. This group was leading people by foot across the Alps.

Hans went to Salzburg and showed the note to a couple of guys who were the head of the Zionists there. Hans had been told they would help them. The guys went wild and started cussing.

"I just met Peter and Jimmy. I thought they were friends of yours," Hans explained.

This conflict and misunderstanding did not disrupt Hans' persistence. He didn't give up. He visited the Zionist group everyday. He knew that this group decided who would go.

After figuring out the politics of the organization, Hans told them he had a brother in Palestine. He and his mother wanted to be reunited with his brother. The Zionists didn't verify his story. They gave them the papers.

Hans and Camilla journeyed across the Alps with a group of 50 people destined to get through the Austrian Alps illegally to Italy. They crossed many steep mountains. At one point, Camilla was at the top of a steep mountain that she had to climb down. Her head was spinning. She said, "I'm not moving. There's nothing here but ice and snow."

Hans was holding the two oil paintings from their home in Cieszyn in a briefcase. He put Camilla on top of the briefcase and gave her a shove. She slid safely down the hill.

CHAPTER 14

Italy

Once they arrived in Italy, they went to a refugee camp supported by the United Nations Refugee Rehabilitation Administration (UNRRA). They administered camps for thousands of displaced persons after the war.

Life seemed much better.

The Zionists, however, wanted everyone at the camps to go to Palestine as soon as possible. They didn't care whether the British caught them. Their mission was to demonstrate that all Jews wanted to go to Palestine. This movement emphasized the need for an all-Jewish state—Israel.

Hans and Camilla started researching opportunities in Milan. They learned that the Jewish American Distribution Committee (JOINT), part of the Jewish Federation, was giving scholarships and helping immigrants to get scholarships.

Hans succeeded in obtaining a scholarship to study political science, specializing in eastern European affairs and eastern European languages. This offered assurance that the Zionists couldn't force him to go illegally to Palestine.

Camilla did concerts sponsored by the JOINT in Italy. At first she performed for Jewish refugees with a tenor named Moteo deHoran. (Hans still has half of the program distributed at this concert).

Then she went on another concert tour with an Israeli ballerina Chasa Levy all over Italy.

In 1946, she played in a small chamber orchestra.

Hans also took private singing lessons in Milan.

From 1945-1950, Hans and Camilla stayed in Milan while Hans earned his Ph.D.

While they were there, Hans became involved with a gal named Toby. She was from Romania (formerly Hungary). She had also survived the concentration camps. She told stories about how she had been asked to march around naked in Auschwitz. Dr. Mengele would point his finger at those who would go the gas chamber.

Toby's five uncles (brothers of her late mother residing in America) sent her money to care for her lavishly. All the money couldn't help her condition however. She had a spot on her lungs. The fear of tuberculosis was so intense at that time; everyone had to pass a health inspection before they could emigrate to America.

In 1949, the majority of the Jews in Italy were emigrating to Israel or America, wherever they had relatives.

Since Topy couldn't pass the health inspection to go to America, she and her sister decided to go to Israel.

Toby wrote to Hans from Israel a few times. There was a shortage of places to live, especially for people without money. Fortunately, Toby and her sister Ester were still receiving financial help from their uncles in the United States. This money helped them survive their first year in Israel.

In 1950, Hans was working in Naples at a refugee hospital administered by the International Refugee Organization (IRO). At that time HIAS, a Jewish organization, helped obtain papers for refugees with families to go to America. With the help of HIAS, Hans and Camilla arranged to be transported to America by boat. They obtained the appropriate papers and were ready to sail.

CHAPTER 15

America

They traveled on a former military boat called General Hershey for a nine-day voyage. Although the weather was nice for two or three days, it was stormy most of the time. Many of the passengers were seasick. Luckily, Camilla and Hans were in good shape. They enjoyed gorging on the food. By American standards, it was just Navy food. To Hans and Camilla it seemed like delicacies after all the years of hunger.

On Sept. 12, 1950, they finally arrived in New York. It was the second day of Rosh Hashanah, the Jewish New Year. They thought that was a good omen to arrive on this High Holy Day for a new beginning in a new country.

After all the formalities—an ID check and completing some paperwork—were completed, a representative of the American Distribution Committee took them to a hotel and told them that within 48 hours they would probably be transported to Cleveland, Ohio, their future home.

"We could have changed our destination if we wanted to, but since we didn't know anybody anywhere anyhow, we decided to go there," Hans said.

They had been told that Cleveland was a big industrial city with lots of possibilities. There was another couple with them, the Milchikers, a young couple with one child, and Alice Wessel from Yugoslavia with her daughter Pat (who was about 19 years old) who Hans and Camilla had met in Italy. The Wessels were destined to go to Akron. The Milchikers had relatives in Cleveland, so they were also on their way there.

After about 24 hours in New York, they were told that within a couple hours someone would pick them up in a taxi and take them to the railroad station. From there they'd go to Cleveland. They should be ready with all their things packed. They spent about 12 hours on a train. It was a boring voyage.

CHAPTER 16

Cleveland

When they arrived in Cleveland, a young lady from the Jewish Family Services was waiting for them. They went to lunch. Hans volunteered to pay, and the social worker accepted the treat. Then they took a taxi and drove through the worst part of Cleveland, which left a horrible impression. After living for so many years in beautiful Italy, Cleveland initially seemed terrible. She took them to a house where Jewish Family Services had rented a room for them for a month. Hans and Camilla had one bedroom and shared the kitchen and the bathroom with the owner of the home, an elderly Jewish lady. They lived there for a few months until they were able to get halfway decent jobs.

The Jewish Family Service and the Jewish Vocational Service did only the bare minimum, which meant very, very little. The rest was up to the immigrants.

Fortunately, Camilla and Hans both spoke English. Unfortunately, they arrived near the end of the Korean War and the former American service men had just returned home and were also looking for jobs. This made it more difficult for the newcomers to find jobs close to their skill and education level. At the beginning, Hans had manual jobs as a shipping clerk and a bus boy, and Camilla worked as a dairy clerk.

After three or four months, they finally found an apartment. This was difficult due to a shortage of rental properties. They bought their first furniture on credit and started a more-or-less normal life.

In 1952, Hans and Camilla both had fairly good jobs. Hans started working for J & L Jones and Laughlin Steel Co., where he was employed for 31 years. He held many different jobs in various capacities at the company. He retired as director of purchasing.

That same year, he bought his first brand new Chevy and met his future wife, Renee Globus, at a musical party.

A friend invited Hans to meet a single woman friend of his. Hans really didn't want to go, but didn't want to disappoint his friend. When Hans met her, he was not attracted to her.

As he mingled with the other guests, he met Renee.

After meeting at the party, they started to date. They discovered that they had lots in common, mainly a love for music, the theatre, the arts and each other. They were engaged in 1953, and they were married in 1954.

In 1955, there was a flicker of hope of receiving some compensation for the confiscated property.

Hans read in the newspaper that there was a possibility of receiving compensation from the Polish government for nationalized real estate and industry. Poland paid the United States $40 million to compensate American citizens who lost property in Poland. Hans wrote to the Foreign Claims Commission in the U.S. Department of Justice in Washington, D.C., and received all the forms. Hans sent in a claim, but it was denied. He received a response saying that he had no right to these reparations since he was not a U.S. citizen when the factory was confiscated in 1946. These funds were for people who were American citizens at the time of nationalization in 1945 and 1946. At that time he was a Polish citizen, so he didn't qualify. All of these funds were allocated.

For a long time, he didn't make any further attempts to regain the factory or even think about it. Hans and Camilla tried to forget about the past. Once upon a time, there was a chocolate wafer factory owned by the Schrameks. That was it. They started to feel like there was nothing to regain.

Hans pursued his singing hobby. He sang semiprofessionally from 1957-80. He sang as a tenor soloist in Cleveland's First

Congressional Church for five years and as a choir soloist at several synagogues. He also performed in several ethnic programs since he sang in many languages. He formed a duo with Betty Lustig, Renee's best friend since grade school. Betty arranged different songs. She sang and accompanied him on piano and guitar. They performed for the Russian Cultural Club and performed in Hebrew and Yiddish for many Jewish groups.

Renee worked for the accounting department of the Navy as a supervisor until she got pregnant. They bought their first house in May 1960 on Revere Road in Cleveland Heights. Moving and decorating the new home gave them a lot of pleasure and occupied their free time. On November 23 of that same year, their son, Bradley, was born.

Camilla had a small apartment near Hans, Renee and Bradley. Camilla took care of Bradley when Hans and Renee went on vacation. The family remained very close. Camilla taught Bradley how to play piano when he was very young.

Camilla became ill in 1965. She had a hemorrhoids operation, which they hoped would cure her. But the operation had a traumatic impact on her. She sank deeper and deeper into a depression. There was nothing they could do. The doctor gave her electric shocks, which didn't help. Hans watched her decline. She just wanted to die. In 1967, she had a major stroke and passed away an hour later.

Hans was saddened by his mother's death. This was very difficult for Hans to accept since they had been extremely close his entire life. His mother was his last link to his past, except the two paintings that Hans carried with him across the Alps. These paintings are hanging on the family's living room wall.

In 1978, Hans was in a car accident and almost lost his voice. He was hospitalized for hiccups that lasted for two weeks. His voice came back, but he had problems singing. He had to decline future singing offers.

Then he started concentrating on his second hobby—collecting antiques. He and Renee started traveling and buying and exchanging antiques. The entire family, including Bradley, learned about old jewelry and other collectibles.

They continued to pursue this hobby by participating in regional flea markets. Occasionally, they would apply their knowledge of antiques and collectibles to supervising estate sales for people in the community.

In the meantime, Bradley graduated from The Ohio State University in Columbus, Ohio, where he earned bachelor's and master's degrees. Then he met Lynn Gottlieb in 1986 and married in 1989.

CHAPTER 17

Best friends

During Hans' years in Italy and later in the United States, he found that four of his best friends, who had been in the Soviet Union during WWII, had survived the Holocaust.

Hans' childhood friend, Ricky Stamberger (alias Jake Lancer) and the other boys had joined the army formed under the command of General Andlers in the Soviet Union near the Persian border to fight Hitler's army. Later this army left the Soviet Union and fought together with the allies against Hitler in Italy and Africa.

After the war, they were allowed to stay and study in England. Ricky lived in Israel for awhile and later immigrated to Australia where he made a wonderful life for himself and his family. He realized the Jewish dream. He and his wife have two sons. One is a lawyer, and the other is a doctor. He has at least six grandchildren.

Hans thought his other three friends Bruno Adler, Emil Klein and Ernest Hornung were in England until he heard from Emil.

In 1967 Hans, Renee and Bradley were sitting in the kitchen when the phone rang. Renee answered. After a couple words, she said, "Hans, I think it's for you."

He took the receiver. To his great surprise, it was his friend Emil. He was calling from the United States where he had lived since 1948. He lived on Long Island in New York with his family and had a very prosperous business. He insisted that Hans come to see him. After a few months, Hans went and visited Emil, his wife Heddy and their children. Since then, they have reestablished their friendship.

Later, Hans heard that Menek Hirschhorn, the accountant at the factory who had been so kind to his family, survived the war and moved to England. Hirschhorn had started a wholesale business that sold blankets and sweaters made out of Creagoran wool. Bradley visited Hirschhorn in 1979 when he was in England on a school tour. Hans also had a reunion with him in 1975 and 1976.

Hans had his first reunion with Ricky in the 1970s in New York City. Hans realized that the factory was still in operation when he purchased an Olza wafer while walking around with Ricky in New York. The wafer was embossed with the Bracia Schramek emblem, which proved that Olza was still using the original equipment.

Hans and Ricky had another reunion in 1990 in Washington, D.C. Since both of them were retired at that time, they were relaxed and reflected about past, present and future plans. They felt lucky to be alive.

PART III
Reclaiming the factory

CHAPTER 18

1992

As communism began to crumble with the Berlin Wall, the movement toward a democratic regime gained momentum in Poland.

In 1991, his son Bradley began to urge Hans to try to regain ownership of the factory. Bradley had read an article in the *Columbus Dispatch* indicating that former Ohio Governor Richard Celeste was trying to encourage Americans to invest in Warsaw Pact nations—Poland, Hungary and Czechoslovakia. These countries would need many goods and services in order to enter the free-market economy of the West.

Bradley called Celeste who recommended that he call the Polish Embassy. Krzysztof Kroveski at the embassy said there's "no chance" of reclaiming the factory. It would be a "waste of time for a lawyer." He indicated that the Polish government wants to stop reprivatization because it is swamped with similar claims. The ministry had not decided how to handle them.

At first Hans didn't want to relive his past. He wanted to forget about it. But Bradley was very aggressive about pursuing this. Reluctantly, Hans agreed to try to regain the factory.

Just before Hans retained an attorney, his cousin Professor Dr. Alfred "Aldi" Schramek, Wilhelm's son—who now lives in Israel—called Hans from San Francisco where he was vacationing. Aldi who had always aspired to be a medical doctor and had never been interested in the factory as a child or adult, all of a sudden was interested in reclaiming his share of the factory.

"Hans, I just hired a lawyer in Israel to regain grandmother's building and the factory. Would you like to participate with me?" Aldi asked.

Since Hans hadn't hired a lawyer yet, he agreed.

Hans sent Aldi a power of attorney authorizing Asher Weissberg, Aldi's Israeli attorney, to represent his interests along with Aldi's.

Hans' friends and acquaintances from Cieszyn also offered to help him regain the factory.

Hans' friend Bruno cut out an ad from the *London Financial Times* on Sept. 22, 1992. The ad announced that Olza stock is for sale.

The ad said:

REPUBLIC OF POLAND

The Minister of Privatisation acting on behalf of the State Treasury, in accordance with the Privatisation Law (Article 23, 13 July 1990) invites interested parties to negotiations for the acquisition of (not less than 10%) share in OLZA S.A.

The company is a manufacturer of confectionery products:
* Chocolate covered wafer bars (Prince Polo brand)
* Wafer bars
* Prince candy bars
* Chocolate covered nuts and raisins

The Company is located in Cieszyn in Southern Poland; it employs 800 people and had sales of USS$21 mln in 1991. In accordance with the Privatisation Law (Article 24) up to 20% of shares will be offered to company's management and employees on preferential terms.

For further information on how to obtain the Information Memorandum please contact the advisor acting on behalf of the Ministry of Privatisation:

Central Europe Trust Co. Ltd.

Andre Mierzwa, Project Directory

ul. Parkingowa 1

fax. (48 22) 21 75 73

The deadline for accepting written proposals is 14 October 1992. The Minister of Privitisation reserves the right to cancel this invitation and not to take up negotiations without giving reasons.

CENTRAL EUROPE TRUST

Hans and Aldi were furious. How could the Polish government sell OLZA stock when it didn't rightfully own the company?

Weissberg immediately contacted the Ministry of Privatisation in Poland and informed them that there are still heirs to this business and the real estate connected with it. He tried to stop the stock offering.

Weissberg then made arrangements with a Polish attorney, Mgr. Jadwiga Wojnar, to claim ownership of Hermina's building and their fathers' factory.

Wojnar's initial research reflected that Hans is the only legal heir to the factory. She couldn't find any documentation verifying Aldi's claim. Wilheim Schramek was not included as co-owner in any of the existing books. Only Bruno Schramek—deceased in 1932—appeared in the books as the sole owner.

Wojnar found that Julius Pietschmann was listed as buying the factory from Bruno Schramek during the war in 1943.

"That Nazi lied," Hans said. "How could he have bought the land from my father in 1943 when my father died in 1932?"

Wojnar agreed and marched to the courthouse. She had the two entries annulled. Pietschmann's name was removed from the record book and Bruno's name was re-entered.

After months of not hearing anything from Weissberg, Hans decided to write a letter to him requesting information.

Weissberg never answered. Hans made a copy of the letter and gave it to Aldi.

Since Hans was paying Weissberg, he felt that he was entitled to be informed about the case. Weissberg was not keeping Hans informed.

When Aldi and Weissberg weren't responsive, Hans grew suspicious. He remembered his Uncle Wilhelm's behavior. Any relative who could leave his nephew to be captured apparently couldn't have many scruples. "Like father, like son?" Hans wondered.

Aldi did, however, communicate about how he felt any claim proceeds should be divided. He asked Hans to split the money equally three ways among himself and Claudia (Aldi's brother Rolf's widow) even though they should be entitled to only 50% since Bruno and Wilhelm were 50-50 partners.

When Aldi finally sent Hans copies of Weissberg's correspondence, Hans became even more suspicious and aggravated. His name was not mentioned in any of the letters. All the correspondence mentioned only Alfred Schramek as Weissberg's client. Hans didn't think that Weissberg was representing his interest in an acceptable manner.

He wrote to Aldi threatening to revoke his power of attorney if things didn't change. He demanded that Weissberg recognize him as a client and respond immediately to his list of questions and requests.

When Weissberg didn't respond for four weeks, Hans called Aldi and gave him a final warning that he wasn't satisfied with Weissberg's services. If he didn't receive a satisfactory response to his requests, he would revoke his power of attorney.

Aldi assured him that Weissberg had every intention of meeting his demands.

Hans and Renee prepared to move to Florida for the winter. Aldi called Hans on the day he left for Florida in December 1992. Aldi had just returned from Tel Aviv where he had talked to Weissberg. Aldi assured Hans that Weissberg would get in touch with him within the next two weeks. Four weeks passed, and Hans didn't hear anything.

From Florida, Hans called Aldi to inform him that he hadn't heard from Weissberg, and he was planning to fire him. Again Aldi begged Hans to call Weissberg and talk to him. Maybe there is a misunderstanding. Maybe the mail is on the way. So Hans called Weissberg. The conversation convinced him that Weissberg had no intention of answering his questions and that he had accomplished practically nothing. He hadn't even sent his power of attorney to Wojnar in Poland, as she had requested. Hans fired him on the phone.

CHAPTER 19

1993

Hans called Wojnar, the Polish attorney employed by Weissberg, and asked her to represent him directly.

"Are you in conflict with Aldi?" she asked.

"No," Hans responded.

"I will represent you if Aldi sends me a letter stating that there is no litigation between the two of you."

"How much will it cost? May I pay you on a contingency basis?"

"We do not accept contingency payments," she said. "The fee to represent you will probably be less than this toll call," she said.

Wojnar told Hans that she had been having difficulty obtaining information from Weissberg. She had not received Hans' power attorney or the notarized copy of Camilla's death certificate that Weissberg was supposed to forward to her several months ago. She agreed to send Hans another power of attorney form for his signature. Hans promised to resend Camilla's death certificate directly to her.

She would also send him an estimate of how much her services would cost.

They proceeded to discuss the case.

"The government owns the machinery and the business, because evidently it was legally nationalized under Polish law," she said.

"What about the property, such as the two three-story buildings, in which the factory is contained?" Hans asked.

"We can try to reclaim the buildings and the land," she replied.

"What about the orchard?" Hans asked.

"It is no longer there. They expanded the factory onto that land."

"I want to reclaim Bracia Schramek—not just the land and real estate. Pietschmann, a former employee of Bracia Schramek, worked in the factory until the day the government took it over. It was a complete factory then—even though new machines might have been added," Hans exclaimed.

"You can't reclaim the factory if it was legally nationalized under Polish law. Since the new democratic government isn't responsible for the communist government, you couldn't charge them for the years when the communists operated the factory. You might be able to charge Olza for using the building for the last couple years," she said.

"You could also sell your grandmother's building. The records show that your family has owned it since the early 1900s," she said.

Wojnar explained that before Hans could file litigation against anyone for taking the real estate or the business—he had to prove that it belongs to him.

Wojnar advised that they begin by proving that Bruno died in 1932 and that Hans is his only legal heir.

After so many years, it would be very hard to find papers. Most of them had been destroyed.

Wojnar said she would go to the Polish magistrate immediately to try to find his father's death certificate.

Hans knew that his father's death certificate had been stored in the House of the Jewish Congregation. The Germans had burned the synagogue and the building adjacent to it, which housed all the congregation's records, including birth and death certificates.

Unfortunately, Bruno's grave stone had been removed from the Jewish Cemetery.

There was a slight chance that Bruno's name was inscribed on the wall of a chapel at the cemetery. The chapel had been destroyed.

Wojnar assured Hans that if the Polish magistrate didn't have a copy of the death certificate, other steps could be taken. They could record depositions that would stand up in court.

To obtain a copy of Bruno's death certificate, a current Polish citizen had to testify to the Administration of Civil Records in Cieszyn. They must verify when Bruno died and confirm that the records had been burned.

Hans asked Wojnar to try to locate people in Cieszyn who knew Bruno and would testify for a deposition.

Hans was still in touch with five or six friends who had known his father well. (Hans could vividly remember seeing his friend Ricky at Bruno's funeral.)

Wojnar said they couldn't testify. Only a current Polish citizen residing in Poland could testify in a Polish court.

Hans mentioned a few other people who might still be living in Poland.

Wojnar tried to locate these people and responded, "She died. He died. She died. I think she's still living," she responded.

Then Hans remembered a woman who worked in the factory and was his governess for two years. "Annie would be about 85 now. She knew my father. She would definitely remember my family. She went to Italy with us when I was young. She appreciated that opportunity very much since she was from a poor family. She was extremely loyal to my family up until 1939," Hans explained.

"Also, another couple may still be alive. He was my uncle's and father's personal driver," Hans said. "He married a woman who cooked for Uncle Wilhelm's family. Perhaps Aldi has their address. I know he corresponded with them for many years."

"I'll try to find them," she said. "Please call me in a month."

Hans called her for an update on her progress. She hadn't found the death certificate. She reminded Hans that she needed a letter from Aldi, confirming that no conflict exists between him and

Hans. If Aldi agrees to provide this in writing then she would represent both of them individually—Hans directly and Aldi through Weissberg.

Hans called Aldi. He agreed again to send Wojnar a letter. Aldi asked Hans for an additional $1,000 to pay Weissberg for his services. Aldi wanted to retain Weissberg until their Grandmother Hermina's property is sold. Hans refused to pay for services he wasn't receiving. Aldi agreed that Weissberg was going in circles and accomplishing very little.

The next time that Hans called Wojnar, they discussed Hermina's building. Wojnar seemed to be contradicting herself.

"Inflation is very high in Poland now," she said. "There is an over abundance of property on the market. We'll need to take what we can get. The property is in ruins."

The next time they talked, she said, "Although the property is in poor condition, the apartments and stores in it are completely occupied."

"This property is in a prime location," Hans said. "If someone tore down the building and made the land into a parking lot, they could make a fortune."

"They can't demolish that property," she said. "Those buildings are historic landmarks."

Then she'd say, "People are willing to buy property," contradicting herself. "They made a night club out of one of the stores located in your property and rented it. Now it is becoming more desirable."

Wojnar received an offer for the building, but they couldn't respond until the proof of ownership was confirmed in writing by the proper authorities.

Then some discouraging news came. *The New York Times* reported that the Polish government voted against privatizing industry in Poland. It sounded like this would impact the factory. Chances of regaining ownership seemed remote.

A few weeks later, however, Emil told Hans that *The New York Times* reported that Jacobs Suchard, a Swiss subsidiary of Philip

Morris, had contracted to buy 80% of the factory for $5 million. The other 20% would belong to the employees of the factory.

The March 1993 article said:

JACOBS SUCHARD TAKING CONTROL OF
POLISH COMPANY

Jacobs Suchard A.G., a subsidiary of the Philip Morris Companies, signed an agreement yesterday to buy 80 percent of the Polish confectioner Olza S.A. for more than $5 million. Suchard, the Swiss-based chocolate and coffee maker, said it would spend $11.3 million to expand capacity at the Cieszyn plant in southern Poland and would make $15 million in long-term investments.

Jacobs Suchard pledged to maintain Olza's existing employment level for at least 30 months and to increase wages. Olza, Poland's leading producer of chocolate-covered wafers, had $24 million in revenue last year. Jacobs Suchard, which has plants in 14 counties, reported $4.6 billion in 1992 revenue.

(Reuters)

Evidently, Olza was not affected by the government's decision. Parliament's vote only affected heavy industry and not the chocolate factory.

Hans immediately called Wojnar. She had heard the news on television and was as surprised as the Schrameks.

Hans was excited about the possibility of sharing the proceeds of the sale of the factory with the Polish government. Afterall, the factory belonged to the Schramek family. No one ever compensated the family for it.

Wojnar emphasized that Hans could not file suit with the Polish ministry to reclaim ownership of the factory until he can prove when his father died and that he is the legal heir. The connection of each heir—Hans, Aldi and Claudia, Rolf's widow—must be documented.

She had finally received the letter from Aldi confirming that there is no conflict of interest between him and Hans, so they could proceed. In return, Aldi asked Hans for a letter stating that should Hans get restitution as the only legal heir he would share the net amount after expenses with Aldi in equal parts.

Although Wojnar had reiterated that the documents she had seen indicated that Hans is the only legal heir to the chocolate factory. Hans agreed to share 50% of the money with Aldi and Claudia—not split it three ways, as Aldi previously requested.

As Hans was trying to think of how to prove his legal identity, he remembered the 1945 court case.

"In 1945, my mother and I hired two attorneys. One of them was a probate judge who probated the will in 1932. Uncle Wilhelm was still alive. He sent me a power of attorney so we could make a claim to get the factory back. We lost that suit. Since there was a hearing and a copy of the will was shown to the court, shouldn't that be accessible from the court records?" Hans asked Wojnar.

"Yes. We should be able to obtain those records," Wojnar said. "The court is required to keep cases on file for 50 years."

Hans agreed to send her $175 to cover her costs for obtaining documentation to prove when Bruno died and another power of attorney authorizing her to represent him.

Wojnar said that she planned to go on vacation for a month until May 6, 1993. While she's gone, she'll have a clerk research the court records from 1945-46 to try to find a copy of the will and legal proceedings concerning the factory.

Hans called Wojnar on May 9. She had accomplished nothing. She emphasized that he could only claim the land and the building.

Hans disagreed. His family started the business. When the government took it over, it was a thriving operation. The nucleus of the factory was operating in 1945 and 1946. "I want to reclaim Bracia Schramek!" he exclaimed.

She mentioned that recompensation is only being given to Polish citizens who currently live in Poland. However, that could change.

"I feel like I'm throwing money away," Hans said.

"At the rate we're charging, you're not throwing money away," she assured him. She asked Hans to call her back on May 17.

She finally received Hans' letter, six weeks after he had mailed it. The envelope was damaged. It looked like it had been opened and resealed. Someone had obviously tampered with it. All the contents were there—a letter, check and two powers of attorney.

Five days later, she received a check from Weissberg for Aldi's share of her fee.

On May 17, Wojnar reported that she had found two file numbers from 1945. They listed Camilla and Hans as plaintiffs. The first dealt with Camilla trying to reclaim Hermina's building. The second dealt with Hans trying to regain ownership of the factory. That file probably contained his father's will.

The courthouse had been remodeled, and all the files were moved to various locations. The custodian at the courthouse agreed to help her find the files. They're required to keep them for 50 years, so they must be there. The custodian dug through the dirt and mud looking for the right box.

Hans asked, "What if you can't find the files? Will you continue to try to find someone to testify for a deposition, so we can reconstruct the death certificate?"

She replied that she's hoping to find a copy of the will in the court records. If she does, the deposition would be unnecessary. She was optimistic that the files would contain something helpful.

Hans said he'd call back in two weeks. If they haven't found the will, they would proceed to reconstruct the death certificate.

"Could you come to Cieszyn after we have the proper documentation?" she asked Hans. "It would be helpful when we're ready to sell your grandmother's building. I can handle this matter with a power of attorney, but would appreciate it if you would come and help."

"My wife, Renee, and I will come when it is time to close on the sale of Grandmother Hermina's building," Hans replied.

Later that day, when Hans shared this conversation with his son, Bradley asked, "Why don't you go to Cieszyn now?"

"Going there now would be a waste of time and money," Hans replied. "It would cost at least $650 to fly there, plus room and board. It would be very costly to stay there for two or three weeks."

Hans was somewhat skeptical.

"Nobody in Poland is to be trusted," he told Bradley. "Wojnar said she has a few other Jewish clients who are American. But I still feel that she might be resentful, because I am a Jew who was wealthy and trying to get money back," he said.

Hans often wondered whether Wojnar was his friend or the Polish government's. It was hard to tell with so many miles between them.

"It seems like it's taking so long," Bradley said.

"We have to follow the law. If the law requires a death certificate, we have to have a death certificate. I didn't tell her about the court proceedings in 1945 and 1946 until March. It takes time. Since then she was on vacation for a month," Hans said.

"By the way, Aldi's lawyer, Weissberg, informed her that he was coming the first of May, but she didn't hear from him," Hans added. "I wasn't surprised that Weissburg was unreliable. I am glad to be working directly with Wojnar."

Hans talked to Wojnar again on June 2, 1993. They hadn't found anything. The custodian had searched for weeks in the dirt before giving up. Since the court is responsible for losing the files, Wojnar said she would request an official letter from the courts that the files, which probably contained Bruno's death certificate and will, were lost.

In the meantime, she agreed to proceed with the deposition. When she receives the letter from the court and depositions from Polish citizens who knew Bruno, she'll apply for another copy of Bruno's death certificate.

Hans made a notarized deposition saying where his family lived in Cieszyn when Bruno died, and he verified that Bruno had no other children. He sent his notarized deposition and a copy of Camilla's death certificate to Wojnar.

Wojnar found the Schramek's former maid, Alojzia Polock, to testify that she worked for the Schramek's and that she attended Bruno's funeral in December 1932.

Bruno's personal chauffeur, Wladyslaw Tomiszek, gave similar testimony.

Once Wojnar obtains the death certificate, she'll take it to probate court to document that Hans is the only heir to the factory.

Hans received a letter from Wojnar on Aug. 18, 1993. She enclosed a photocopy of the decision and a reconstructed legal copy of Bruno's death certificate.

She indicated that she had applied for a court hearing to determine his inheritance from Bruno Schramek, but the court hadn't set a date yet.

Once the court rules that the living heirs may claim Hermina's building, Wojnar will need Aldi's mother's and father's death certificates, as well. All three heirs—Hans, Aldi and Claudia, Rolf's widow—must provide documentation proving their legal rights to the property.

Wojnar wasn't able to contact Claudia. She asked Weissberg, and Hans wrote to Aldi twice asking for help contacting Claudia. If she wants to participate in the claim, she, too, must have legal representation. She would need to sign a power of attorney, so Wojnar could represent her as an heir.

If Claudia doesn't get a Polish representative, the court would be forced to translate everything into English and send a copy to Claudia in Israel. This could delay proceedings for up to a year. If Claudia doesn't want to claim her part ownership of the building, she could either resign or sell her share.

Later in August, Hans received the following letter from Aldi. Hans translated it to English from Polish as follows:

The Ministry of Possession Restructions
00-525 Warsaw, ul.Krucza 36
State Undersecretary
Tel. 628 0281, Fax: 213 361 625114
Tlx. 816 521
DPU/1805/93
DM/298/93
Warsaw, March 3, 1993
Mr. Asher Weissberg
Weissberg and Ben Porat Law Offices and Notary
Tel-Aviv, Israel
Fax: 972 3 566 1951
Dear Sir:

In regard to your letter sent to Central Europe Trust Co. LTD., advisors to the Ministry of Possessional Restructions RE: ZPC Olza S.A. from October the 8th, 1992, I am kindly informing you, that in the present law structure, there is no basis to come forward by the former owners with claims (except article 156, paragraph 1, pt. 2 kpa) or to accept those claims.

In the light of accessable documents, one can assume that the Schramek family owned the prewar factory of sugar wafers, cookies and chocolate "OLZA and not Julius Pitchman, who bought this factory in 1943 from the Germans, being before this date, the trustee and superintendent of said factory, designated by the occupational government.

In accord with the law of nationalization, all activities or laws governing this enterprise from 1 September 1939, were by the law annulled.

The sugar wafer, cookie and chocolate factory OLZA was taken over as the property of the state (Feder. Goverm) in accordance with regulation 3 of the law from January 3, 1946, about the take over as state property of basic branches of national industry.

According to the writings of this decree, the owners were supposed to receive recompensation, which however has not been

*paid, because the advisory council of ministers failed to make
proper decisions and laws.*

*As soon as a legal basis will exist to satisfy the claims of the
former owners, it will be the federal treasury to take care of this.*

*In case, for different reasons, should it become impossible to
satisfy the claimants with hard cash, the decree of reprivatization forsees other ways of recompensation like another property
or reprivatization bonds.*

*At the same time, the decree forsees as a lawful claimant a
Polish citizen, residing in Poland, or a person living abroad, if
he or she claims his rights within the time prescribed by law and
then acquires Polish citizenship and will make his residence in
Poland.*

*Taking all the above into consideration, one has to ac-
knowledge, that at this time there are no reasons which would
make it impossible to privatize ZPC OLZA SA.*

Respectfully,
Jerry Sterniecki
for the Undersecretary of State

Since they were so close to obtaining the necessary documentation, Hans decided to write a letter to Jacob Suchard, as follows:

August 10, 1993
TO: Fa. Jacobs–Suchard
2003 Neuchatel
Switzerland
RE: Factory OLZA, S.A. Cieszyn, Poland.

*Gentlemen, I, Hans Schramek, of 2069 Revere Road,
Cleveland, Ohio 44118, U.S.A., am the only son and rightful
heir of the late Bruno Schramek, cofounder and owner of the
sugar wafer and chocolate factory "Bracia Schramek, TIP-TOP,
Cieszyn, Poland."*

This factory has been nationalized in 1945, over the

protest of the rightful owners, renamed to Factory OLZA S.A.
by the Communist regime.

    After the collapse of said regime in Poland, my cousin Prof.
Dr. Alfred Schramek and I claimed this factory as our rightful
inheritance.

    It came to our knowledge, from an announcement in the
New York Times of March 1993, that Jacobs—Suchard, a sub-
sidiary of Philip Morris, made an agreement with the Polish
Government to purchase 80% of this factory now known as
OLZA S.A. Cieszyn.

    I would be obliged to you if you would let me know if this
purchase was consummated, and, if so, under what conditions.

    Thanking you in advance for conveying to me this infor-
mation.

I remain sincerely yours,
Hans Schramek

Wojnar sent a packet of information to Hans.

She sent him a power of attorney to represent him in reclaiming Hermina's building. This appears to be fairly simple. Wojnar
will charge $200 for this service. Hans agreed to proceed with
this.

Secondly, Wojnar discussed the factory.

There are two real estate parcels on Liburnia Street where the
factory is located. In the record book, there are two entries—one
for the ground and the buildings built on that ground and the
other for the ground that up until 1939 was an orchard adjoining
the factory.

According to court records, Pietschmann went to court and
became the owner. This had been recently annulled because the
transaction occurred during the war, and he was a Nazi. He couldn't
have legally purchased the property from Bruno Schramek in 1943,
because Bruno died in 1932. He had just taken over the Jewish
property. The entry was declared illegal.

Wojnar explained that since the Communists took over the factory in accordance with Polish law, the Schramek's hands are tied until the Polish government passes a law saying how to recompensate for industry confiscated during the war.

Wojnar also looked up the decision to nationalize the factory.

A factory that employed at least 50 workers on each shift had to be nationalized. Therefore, she would like Hans to inform her if the factory could have possibly employed less than 50 people in 1946-47.

If it could be found that the factory employed less than 50 people on each shift, only then could she make a motion to annul the decision by which the factory was nationalized, as not complying with the law of nationalization. This would be the only way to reclaim the factory.

Hans is unable to say how many people were employed in 1945 and 1946.

He knows that the factory worked in three shifts and employed 500 people in 1939. He assumes that in 1945 and 1946, they had no shortage of raw materials and none of the machinery had been transferred to other factories. In which case, they had to employ at least 50 workers on each shift.

To prove that the factory was illegally nationalized in 1946 would be futile.

On the other real estate parcel, with its separate record number in the still existing county real estate record book, OLZA constructed a large factory building. Looking from the front of the street, it was on the left side of the original factory buildings.

This parcel, which was the Schramek's orchard until 1939, had not been nationalized. Despite OLZA's attempt to gain legal possession of the land in 1990, the court's decision is illegal, because it was directed against Pietschmann who never legally owned the land. She could go to court and renew that case and force OLZA to go to court against the Schrameks as the owner of the land.

Wojnar predicted that OLZA would win such a court case again. OLZA had occupied this real estate for over 30 years, which is all that the civil law demands.

Chances of the court ruling in Hans' favor are nil. To represent Hans in these proceedings, Wojnar would charge $400.

Such a court case would bring certain confusion, because OLZA would have to realize that not everything could be obtained that easily.

Since Wojnar was skeptical about reclaiming the real estate, Hans didn't think it would make sense to spend $7 million zloty's—only to confuse the directors of the OLZA factory.

Wojnar said she would charge $190 to represent him in court to prove that he is the legal heir to Bruno.

As soon as this is completed, he would send her another check to represent him in the inheritance case of his Grandmother Hermina's building.

Meanwhile, Hans' friend purchased a wafer in 1993 that was embossed with Bracia Schramek's TIP TOP logo, which shows that OLZA is still using the Schramek's machines.

Wojnar sent Hans a copy of the document issued by the court stating that Hans is the only heir of Bruno Schramek.

In January 1994, Hans' granddaughter Camilla Ann Schramek was born. Brad and Lynn named her in memory of her great grandmother Camilla.

CHAPTER 20

Hermina's building

In April 1994, the Polish court ruled that Hermina's building should be returned to her heirs — Hans, Aldi and Claudia. They may reclaim Hermina's building, where the factory had its humble beginning.

Claudia gave a power of attorney to Aldi to represent her interest. Hans planned to go to Poland for the closing and to have Wojnar represent him.

Wojnar was able to reclaim the building in August 1994. A friend of hers agreed to manage the building and collect the tenants' rent for a few months until the building was sold.

In September, Wojnar arranged to have the property appraised.

Wojnar placed an advertisement in the newspaper to sell the building and received 11 offers.

No other buildings were for sale in that area. The best offer was from a gentleman named Gorski who lives in Cieszyn and does business in Germany. He offered to pay for the building in Germany.

Aldi said, "Take his offer."

Hans said, "Ask him to also pay the inheritance tax and expenses."

Gorski agreed.

Both Hans and Aldi decided to come to Cieszyn for the closing.

CHAPTER 21

Return to Poland

Hans anxiously anticipated returning to his homeland. He had fond childhood memories mixed with fear from the German invasion.

Hans and Renee left Cleveland for Poland on December 5, 1994 — almost 50 years after Hans had come to America.

After a brief layover in Cincinnati, Ohio, they flew to Frankfort and arrived in Warsaw the afternoon of December 6.

They took a taxi to their hotel in the center of the city. The surrounding buildings were illuminated with neon lights. The city felt even livelier than Times Square to Hans, who hadn't been to his homeland since 1945.

They ate dinner and relaxed. The next afternoon, Aldi called. He had arrived from Israel.

Renee and Hans agreed to walk to the hotel where Aldi was staying. After meeting for 10 minutes, Aldi said, "As far as the house is concerned, I don't have any objections to splitting it 50-50. Afterall, the court decided to do it that way. It seems to be right. Our grandmother had two sons. Since they both died, their sons should divide the proceeds from the building in equal portions. However, should we ever get something from the factory, it should be divided into three parts — one for you, one for me and one for Claudia."

Hans wasn't pleased with this overture. Quite awhile ago, Aldi had said that if they were to receive compensation for the factory, Hans should provide a written statement that they would divide the proceeds in half. Hans had done that. Hans didn't appreciate Aldi starting this meeting by changing his mind. Hans wasn't in the mood to argue.

"Look Aldi. There is nothing to argue about right now. It doesn't look like we'll ever get anything for the factory. So why argue about it?" Hans replied.

"I want to set it straight for the record," Aldi said.

"Well, if you want to set it straight for the record. It is going to be 50-50," Hans said.

Hans had already bought three train tickets from Warsaw to Bielsko where they were supposed to meet their lawyer. Wojner had called Hans the day that they arrived. She and Gorski would meet them.

The three of them boarded the train. It was difficult to squeeze through the narrow corridors on the train with their heavy luggage. Some other passengers helped them.

Within about four hours, they were in the city of Bielsko. When they got off the train, Wojnar met Aldi right away. A younger man, Gorski, was beside her. They both helped Hans and Renee with their luggage. Aldi went with Gorski, and Renee and Hans rode with Wojnar to Cieszyn.

After driving for about five minutes, Wojnar said, "Everything has been arranged. Tomorrow morning at about 9:30, come to my office in the courthouse. We will go pay the taxes. Mr. Gorski gave me a down payment that we can use. We will deduct it at the closing. Tomorrow afternoon at 3:30, you will sign the contract with the notary. On Sunday, you will go with Mr. Gorski to Austria to his bank and do the rest," Wojnar said.

"What if we sign the contract in Poland and then he doesn't pay us in Austria?" Hans asked.

"I don't really know the man personally," she said. "I know of him. He has a fairly good reputation. I don't think he would do that, but I can't guarantee," she said. "At least he is paying in dollars outside of Poland."

Wojnar had misled him. Weeks before they came to Poland, Hans had asked Wojnar over the phone whether it was legal to transfer funds out of Poland. She said yes. It's difficult, but it can be done. It takes a long time and some people must be bribed, but it can be done."

Now Wojnar had a different story. "It's almost impossible to take money out of Poland. You don't have to sell to Mr. Gorski. But if you sell to another buyer, they'll give you zloties. True you can buy dollars on any street corner, but nobody will have that much money. Trying to exchange that much money would be very suspicious," Wojnar said.

Also, you owe me some money. Wojnar asked for an additional $1,000 for taking over the house. Hans didn't understand why she wanted this additional money since he had already paid for each step that she had completed for him. Wojnar's friend who had managed the property for the past few months had been paid from the rents she collected. Hans didn't want to make any waves with Wojnar. He was concerned that she could make an anonymous phone call and tell the government that he planned to take money out of Poland. Hans agreed to pay the $1,000.

When they arrived at the hotel in Cieszyn, Hans met with Aldi.

"Did Mr. Gorski tell you about the change in plans?" Hans asked.

"Yes, he told me," Aldi replied.

"Well, what are we going to do?" Hans asked.

"The plan is tomorrow morning to meet with Mrs. Woynar and pay the taxes. In the afternoon, we will sign the contract," Aldi said.

"Where's the guarantee that he's going to pay us?" Hans asked.

"First let's put the luggage in the room. Let's have something to eat. I invited Mr. Gorski, his wife and Mrs. Wojnar to have supper with us in the hotel restaurant," Aldi said.

After supper, the five of them went to Hans' room. They discussed everything very quietly — concerned that the walls had ears. They decided they didn't have a way out.

If they refused to sell the building now, they would still be responsible for its upkeep. The building is falling apart. The city could require them to bring it up to current building codes.

Hans concluded that he wanted to think about it overnight.

"Please don't have a sleepless night over this. You can depend on me. I won't do any tricks. I definitely will pay you the amount that I offered," Gorski said.

So they tentatively agreed on selling the building and trusting that Gorksi would pay them the agreed upon amount in Austria.

During the night, Hans and Aldi were thinking about it. In the morning, they said the situation is unacceptable. They don't know Gorski from Adam. How could Wojnar wait until the last minute to tell them like this?

They discussed their concerns with Ms. Wojnar on their way to pay their taxes. If Mr. Gorski wanted to con us, he would make a good impression.

"I have an idea. He has two cars. One car is worth 600 million zloties. It's a brand new Audi. Let him give us this car as collateral," Wojnar said.

Hans and Aldi didn't like this idea. If Gorksi gave them the key to his car, what guarantee would they have that his wife wouldn't take the car with another key?

Although they were still concerned about the arrangement, they went to pay the taxes. They decided to meet Wojnar at 3 p.m. — 30 minutes before the meeting with Mr. and Mrs. Gorksi and the notary to see if she could think of any other ideas.

That afternoon, Hans, Renee and Aldi walked around Cieszyn. Hans reacquainted himself, and introduced Renee, to his hometown.

Throughout the afternoon, they thought about what they should do.

They returned to meet with Wojnar at 3 p.m.

"I think that I have a solution," she said.

"What is it?" Hans asked.

"At 3:30 p.m. today, we will make a preliminary contract that says that you will sell the building to Mr. Gorski, if he will pay the amount due to you within the next three to four days," she said. "Then you will return to Cieszyn and sign a final contract, and we will close the deal."

"This sounds good," Hans said. "So on Sunday we will go to Austria with Mr. Gorski."

Aldi decided not to go with Mr. Gorski. He will take a taxi to Warsaw and fly to Vienna, where he will rent a car and drive to the small town where Gorski's bank is located and meet them there.

"Why don't you just rent a car in Cieszyn and follow us?" Hans asked.

"I already have an airline ticket from Warsaw to Vienna," Aldi replied. He wouldn't explain why.

On Sunday, very early in the morning, Aldi took a taxi to Warsaw.

Gorski arrived at the hotel after breakfast at about 8:30 a.m. Hans and Renee drove with him through Czechoslovakia toward Austria.

Gorski told them, "Each time you cross the border from Poland to Czechoslovakia, you have to declare how much money you have on you. They have the right to count your money."

The first time they crossed the border, they sat in the car. The border police checked their passports. They declared their belongings. They didn't open their baggage. They didn't ask them to count the money. Somehow Gorski had taken care of everything.

During the six-hour trip to Austria through Czechoslovakia, Gorski told them, mostly in Polish and a little bit in German, "The situation has reversed itself," he said. "You didn't trust me, which I sort of understood, since you didn't know me. But now I am in a situation, where I might mistrust you. You are asking me to give you the money before you sign the final contract," Gorski said.

"We are two old people. Where could we go?" Hans replied.

"Anything could happen. I will only tell you one thing. If you disappear, I will find you. There is no place where you can hide from me," Gorski threatened them.

"Don't be concerned. We wouldn't think of running away," Hans assured him.

"You know my father-in-law is a native of Cieszyn. He told me some old stories about your family. Someone from your family took a large amount of money from the factory and disappeared. The employees at the factory weren't paid for awhile," Gorski said.

Hans knew he was referring to his Uncle Wilhelm.

When they arrived in Shaerding, Austria, Aldi met them at the bank. Aldi said he's going straight back to Vienna and then flying directly to Israel. He had no intentions of returning to Poland.

Hans was worried about going back through Polish customs. He and Renee had been planning to fly from Warsaw to New York and then on to Cleveland. But now they were concerned that customs officials in Warsaw might ask them about the money they collected from the building.

"Tell them you were drinking and you had a good time," Gorksi said.

"Let's be realistic. No matter how much I was drinking and how good of a time I had, there is no way to spend that amount of money," Hans said.

"I will ask my lawyer. Maybe he'll have a suggestion for us," Gorksi said.

After meeting at the bank, Hans and Renee checked into a lovely hotel.

In the meantime, Gorksi went to Germany to meet with his partner. He had an apartment on the Austrian and German border.

Hans spent the evening debating about what to do. He felt there was no way out. He knew that if he accepted the money, he would have to go back to Poland to sign the contract and then go back to Warsaw. This could be very dangerous. If they were caught, they could arrest Hans for taking the money out of Poland.

Being strangers, they would have no one to help them. Hans could speak Polish, but that wouldn't help him. He felt foolish having allowed this situation to have occurred.

On Monday morning, Hans and Renee met with Aldi and then with Gorski. When they arrived at the bank, the money was already prepared.

At the bank they learned they were required to pay a fee to the bank for holding the money for three months. Gorski said that actually he had lost money on the deal. He had prepared the money for them in October. Then, the closing date was delayed because of unpaid mortgages. He had to pay the bank a fee for keeping the money for three months. Hans agreed to split that fee with him. Gorski gave Hans the money, as they had agreed.

Hans transferred most of his money to his bank accounts in the United States and took the balance in cash.

Aldi took all his money in cash and was ready to leave without saying good-bye. Hans caught him.

"Mr. Gorski is advising me to change my travel plans — not to leave from Warsaw, but to leave from Vienna. He will take us to Vienna. From there we will fly to New York," Hans said.

"Okay. If you want to do that, I'll ask Naomi to reserve a room for you," Aldi said and left.

Gorski drove Hans and Renee back to Poland. He warned them to be careful.

"Why are you staying in a hotel in the middle of the city? Everyone can see you there. What if someone else who wanted to buy the building sees you there? They could cause problems for us," Gorski said. "Why don't you stay somewhere outside of the city. There is a brand new hotel that was built especially for university professors and students. The hotel owner is a friend of mine. I will call my wife and see whether she can cancel your reservation at the Rafael Hotel and make a reservation for you at my friend's hotel. No one would pay attention to you right now. A big convention of university professors is coming to Cieszyn. They'll think that you are one of the professors."

He called his wife and told her what to do.

"I think you should change your travel plans. As long as you are in Cieszyn, I can ensure your safety. I will not rest until I know you are safe. After you sign the contract, I will personally take you to Warsaw in my car. But once you are in Warsaw and I leave, something could happen. A copy of the final contract will go to the Treasury Department the day that you sign. Officials from the Treasury Department in Warsaw could ask you for the money," Gorski said.

As he talked, Hans became more worried. Hans translated what Gorski was saying from German to English for Renee.

When they stopped for dinner, Gorksi called his wife. She said that there is no room in the hotel that he suggested, because of the convention of university professors.

Gorski returned to the car.

"Look there are other alternatives. I have a big house," Gorski said. "You could have a private room in my house with a bath-room."

"This is very nice of you, but I would prefer another alterna-tive. I don't want to cramp you or be a burden to you and your family," Hans said.

"No, it wouldn't be a burden," Gorski said. "I would gladly have you over."

"Maybe you can think of something else," Hans responded.

"There is another new American-style hotel that is a little out-side of the city. It is much safer. They have armed guards 24 hours a day. I know all the guards. I am friends with the director of the hotel. Let's see if we can get you a room there," Gorski said.

On the way back, they stopped at that hotel. Gorksi went in. After a few minutes, he came back and said, "You're in luck. The receptionist is an old friend of mine. She has a room for you."

Hans and Renee left their baggage in their hotel room. Gorski took them to his home for some coffee. They continued to discuss their plans. They decided to travel home through Vienna rather than Warsaw. Hans invited Gorski and his wife to have supper with them the next evening in the hotel where they were staying. Gorski drove them back to the hotel.

The next day they had an appointment with Wojnar and then with the notary.

Before they went to sign the final contract at the notary, Hans asked Wojnar whether their account was all settled.

"No," Wojnar replied.

"How could that be? I paid you an additional $1,000 three days ago. That's all we owe you," Hans said.

"I talked to your cousin and found out that he is paying his lawyer 15 percent of the sale of Hermina's building. He told me to collect 50 percent of this amount from Weisberg. I know that I am never going to see that. So, I want to collect 5 percent from you," Wojnar said.

"Ms. Wojnar, I really don't understand. I don't think this is fair. When I hired you, I asked if you were going to work for me on a contingency percentage basis and you said, 'no, we don't work that way in Poland. For everything I do, I'll name a price and you'll send me a check for that amount.' I did that, didn't I?" Hans asked.

"Yes, you always paid the right amount of money on time," Wojnar said.

"Well then, why do you think I should pay more on top of everything else?" Hans asked.

"I feel that I deserve it," Wojnar replied.

The next day, they went to the notary. Hans and Mr. and Mrs. Gorski signed the contract, so the building was legally theirs.

After that Hans went to Wojnar to collect all the papers and settle his account.

"How are we going to settle your salary?" Hans asked.

"I want 5 percent," she said.

Hans paid her the money. Wojnar gave him all the papers. They said good-bye to each other.

Hans and Renee went back to their hotel to meet Mr. and Mrs. Gorski for supper. The next day, Mr. Gorski was to take them to Vienna, if they were able to change their travel plans.

Hans called Warsaw Delta and asked if he could change their plans and fly from Vienna to Cleveland through Kennedy instead of from Warsaw.

"There is only one day that you can do that. Is Dec. 15 okay for you?" she asked.

"Well I would like to leave a little later. Is that all you have?" Hans asked.

"That's all we have," she replied.

"How much is this going to cost me?" Hans asked.

"I don't know off hand. Fax me the first page of your ticket and within 20 minutes I'll let you know," she said. Hans faxed the ticket.

An hour later Hans called her again. Apparently, she didn't receive the fax. Hans faxed it again. Twenty minutes later, she called.

"Two tickets from Vienna will cost you over $1,200," she said.

"Don't pay that much money. Go from Warsaw," Gorski said.

"You told me how dangerous it could be. Money means nothing if it isn't safe," Hans said.

Hans asked Delta to hold the tickets. He will exchange the tickets and pay the difference in Vienna.

In the meantime, Gorski became concerned about the weather. The forecast predicted the temperatures would drop and it would snow in Czechoslovakia and Austria along the route to Vienna.

"Even if I get you to Vienna, I might get caught in the snow storm on my way back to Cieszyn. How about if I take you to a railroad station in Czechoslovakia in the morning before the snow hits? You'll be safe on the train," Gorski said.

"That's not a bad idea," Hans said.

"We have to do something with the papers that you gave me. Those papers are very incriminating. They could get you in trouble. Maybe it would be better if my wife takes the papers over the border to Czechoslovakia in the morning and leaves them with my brother. Then I'll take you there by car to pick them up and you'll take them with you to America," Gorski said.

"That sounds okay," Hans said.

The next day Gorski came to pick them up.

"I thought it over. My brother, who is a customs official, will not be at work today. My wife refused to take the papers. I have a friend who also works at customs. He looked over the papers," Gorski said.

"My God, if they catch you with these papers there would be 10 years for you Mrs. Wojnar and 10 years for Mr. Schramek. Why don't you give me those papers. I'll smuggle them to Czechoslovakia over the holidays when it's safe. Then later you can take the papers to Germany and mail them to Mr. Schramek by certified mail," he said.

Hans agreed and gave him another $350 for that man and to appease Wojnar.

Gorski took Hans and Renee to Czechoslovakia without any problem. Customs officials didn't ask about the money or look in their suitcases. Everything went very smoothly. Gorski had friends all over. As long as they were in Cieszyn with Gorski, Hans felt safe.

Gorski took them to a small town called Carvina where they bought first-class tickets for the train to Vienna. Gorski waited with the Schrameks for two hours for the train in the bitter cold. He helped them with their luggage, embraced and kissed them good-bye and wished them the best. As the train pulled away, Gorski had tears in his eyes.

Hans and Renee arrived in Vienna that afternoon. Hans tried to call Aldi to confirm that Naomi had reserved a room at Hotel Europa. He called several times, but nobody answered. So they decided to take a taxi to the hotel. Luckily, she had reserved a room.

The next morning, they went to Delta.

"Wait a minute while I calculate how much you owe us," the agent said. He calculated over $1,500.

"Suppose we don't have any tickets at all. How much would it cost to get tickets from Vienna to Cleveland for two people? We paid $1,200 for round-trip airfare to Warsaw and back," Hans said. "There must be some kind of mistake."

"Let me recalculate it," the agent said. After spending what seemed like a half hour banging on his computer, finally he said, "Well, give me a check for $300."

Hans gave him $300. The agent gave them the tickets. They went back to the hotel to get their baggage and took a taxi to the airport.

Hans felt fortunate to return safely to American soil.

CHAPTER 22

Restitution for the Factory

During the 1990s, Israel and the European community have been pressuring the Polish government to pass a law that says how Polish citizens, who previously owned nationalized businesses, would be compensated.

The Polish government has been working on a reprivatization act. This law would indicate how the government would compensate the legal owners of nationalized businesses.

A draft of the law developed in 1995 indicated that only Polish citizens could apply for compensation. Since Hans was no longer a Polish citizen, he applied for and received a certificate of Polish citizenship.

In the late 1990s Hans authorized Wojnar to sue the Polish government for illegal nationalization. The suit was denied twice in municipal courts. She appealed. The lawsuit is pending in Poland's Superior Court.

In 1999, a law firm in New York City contacted Hans about participating in a class-action lawsuit against the Polish government. Even though the case would be financed primarily on a contingency basis, Hans initially decided not to participate. However, Hans has been monitoring the class-action lawsuit's progress and the international attention it is receiving.

In June 1999, 11 Polish Jews filed a class-action lawsuit against the Polish government to reclaim their businesses and homes that the Polish government had kept after the defeat of Germany in World War II. The property had been confiscated by the Nazis.

In response to the lawsuit, Poland's cabinet approved a draft of the bill in September 1999 that would provide partial compensation to individuals for property confiscated during World War II and the communist era.

This draft of the bill awards compensation to individuals who have been Polish residents for the past five years. The compensation would be awarded in "reprivatization" bonds. Since Hans has not been a resident of Poland for the past five years, he would not be eligible for compensation the way this draft was written. The Polish government also said it would not adhere to any judgement of a foreign court.

In March 2000, the law firm refiled a revised class-action lawsuit that responded to the Polish government's initial objections (see Appendix).

The Sejm passed a restitution bill on January 11, 2001, and the Senate approved an amended bill on January 26, 2001. The bill explains how the Polish government will compensate individuals for losses due to illegal expropriation of properties from 1944-1962. The Senate removed the citizenship requirement that was included in the Sejm's version of the bill. Before the bill is given to the President, the Sejm must approve the Senate's amendments.

The bill says that owners will get back 50% of the value of their seized property. When possible, the property will be returned in-kind. If the property has already been sold or is in private hands, former owners will receive compensation coupons worth the estimated value of their assets. These coupons could be used to buy state-owned real estate or they could be invested in a specially created investment fund.

The Treasury Ministry has estimated that the introduction of the law will cost the state $11.46 billion. However, government officials have predicted that failure to pass the restitution law could lead to individual claims totaling as much as $66 billion.

President Aleksander Kwasniewski will decide whether to approve or veto the bill in March or April 2001.

With a democratic government now in charge, perhaps the time has come for 50+-year-old claims to be honored.

For a recent update on the class-action case and holocaust restitution in Poland, go to *http://www.holocaustrestitution.com* or e-mail the author of this manuscript at lbscom@frontiernet.net.

CHAPTER 23

Epilogue

Hitler, the communists, and the Polish government have treated Hans and so many others so unfairly that it shouldn't be tolerated. Yet the years continue to pass without justice prevailing.

Hans is currently pursuing his claim to receive compensation for his family's business, which is still producing chocolate and sugar wafers in the 21st century.

Meanwhile, Hans and Renee Schramek are enjoying their retirement. They live in Cleveland, Ohio, during the warm seasons and spend the winters in Florida. Brad, Lynn and Camilla live in Pittsford in upstate New York. Camilla is taking piano lessons, following in her great grandmother Camilla's footsteps.

Occasionally, the family experiences a glimmer of hope that someday Hans will receive some compensation for the factory, as promised in Poland's 1946 nationalization decree.

The story is still unfolding. Perhaps it will have a happy ending sometime in Hans', his wife Renee's, his son Brad's, or his granddaughter Camilla's lifetime.

CHAPTER 24

Appendix

Following is information included in a news release about the class-action lawsuit filed by Mel Urbach and Ed Klein on behalf of Polish Jews who survived the Holocaust or their heirs:

HOLOCAUST VICTIMS SUE POLAND FOR THE RETURN OF THEIR REAL ESTATE

Brooklyn, N.Y. (June 18, 1999)—Eleven Holocaust survivors today filed a class action lawsuit against the Republic of Poland seeking to recover the property their families owned in Warsaw, Krakow, Chestechova, Auschwitz and other Polish towns before the Holocaust.

The lawsuit, filed in Brooklyn Federal District court, seeks to represent tens of thousands of Holocaust survivors and their heirs world wide. Over three million Jews lived in Poland before World War II. Ninety percent were murdered during the Holocaust.

This is the first and largest class action lawsuit brought by Holocaust survivors seeking the return of all the real estate and other assets confiscated from them, during and after the Holocaust. The suit, brought by Mel Urbach and Klein & Solomon, claims that Jewish Holocaust survivors were "unwelcome" in Poland after the Holocaust. Mel Urbach is settlement counsel in the Swiss Banks Case, and is also negotiating a settlement with German industry in the Holocaust slave labor cases.

"There are over three million reasons for filing this law-suit and we appeal to the Pope to persuade Poland to act quickly and fairly with Holocaust victims and heirs" said Mel Urbach, lead Counsel in the case referring to the number of Polish Jews murdered during the Holocaust. Edward Klein, leading Co-Counsel added, "Many of the few who returned to Poland after the war were forced to flee because of a wave of barbaric and violent anti-Semitism. Little was done to protect the Jews. Over 1000 were murdered between 1945 and 1947, and thousands of others were beaten and chased out of Poland."

July 4th will mark the 53rd anniversary of a bloody pogrom in Kielce, Poland, where over 40 Jews were murdered during a day of violence. Immediately after this, droves of Jewish survivors fled Poland. Those intending to return changed their plans and many have vowed never to set foot on Polish soil again. "Rather than being welcomed home as war heros, my clients, the Jewish people, were beaten, threatened, murdered and forced to flee. The Poles said we abandoned our property hardly, after you have spent five years being hunted by the Nazis, you learn not to take any chances. The Poles wanted their country emptied of any Jewish presence. They embarked on a course of racial and ethnic cleansing to ensure that the Jews would flee Poland," Urbach said. Holocaust survivors have only recently gained access to archives throughout Poland. These contain all the necessary documents proving ownership of tens of thousands of valuable parcels of real estate belonging to Holocaust victims.

In prior cases, Swiss and Austrian banks have taken the lead in settling cases with Holocaust victims. German industry is also planning to establish a Fund to compensate World War II era slaves and forced laborers. This fund will also compensate Poles who worked for German industry. Yet, the Polish Government has been slow in passing a law that would allow Jewish Holocaust survivors to reclaim their property. With five to ten Holocaust survivors dying each day time is running out.

For further information contact Mel Urbach at (212) 254-6211 or Ed Klein at (212) 661-9400.

In the following press release, Mel Urbach and Edward Klein discuss the support of the Polish Association of Former Property Owners:

U.S. CLASS ACTION LAWYERS SHOW SOLIDARITY WITH POLISH ASSOCIATION OF FORMER PROPERTY OWNERS

New York, New York (July 1, 1999)—Lawyers, who filed a class action lawsuit against Poland for Holocaust assets, have welcomed an invitation from The Polish Association Of Former Property Owners seeking representation in the case. In a letter last week, Gaspard Krasicki, Chairman of the Association, supported the class action law suit.

The class action lawsuit was filed on June 18, 1999, in Federal Court in Brooklyn and has been assigned to Judge Edward Korman, who helped settle the Swiss banks case for $1.25 billion.

Another major umbrella organization, The All Poland Alliance of Restitution Organizations representing two hundred and fifty thousand Poles whose houses were confiscated by the communist government, will officially endorse and support the lawsuit at a midday press conference in Warsaw on Monday, July 12, 1999. In a phone call on Friday Miroslaw Szypowski, Chairman of the Alliance, asked Mr. Urbach for his assistance and cooperation in their struggle to recover property.

"Just like our other clients in the U.S. and abroad, these people have to live with the helpless feeling that someone else has ownership of their homes," said Mel Urbach, lead counsel in the case. "Buildings have no religion, race nor color, I am honored by the invitation," he added.

Mr. Urbach regretted that he would not be able to attend the Press conference in Warsaw, his firm is arguing against a motion to dismiss in the Slave labor case against Siemans AG this Monday morning in Newark Federal District Court.

Attorneys Edward Klein & Mel Urbach will be visiting survivors and organizations in Poland, England, France and Israel in August. They are also planning to meet representatives of the European Union in their continuing attempts to help in the recovery of assets from World War II.

For further information contact: Mel Urbach at 212.254.6211 or Edward Klein at 800.407.9401.

In September 5, 1999, the following article appeared in the **Jerusalem Post**:

Poland approves compensation for Nazi-seized property
By Marilyn Henry

NEW YORK (September 5, 1999)–Poland's cabinet, in the first step toward the restitution of private property to Nazi victims, has approved a draft bill of "unprecedented scope" that would provide partial compensation to individuals for property confiscated during World War II and the communist era.

The complicated measure, which came six weeks after a class-action lawsuit was filed in New York on behalf of Holocaust survivors to recover private property in Poland, was welcomed as an initial move and also attacked as seriously flawed.

New York attorney Mel Urbach, who filed the suit against Poland, objected to both the valuation of the property and the terms of the payments.

The draft measure offers half of the value of the

property. "Fifty percent is totally unacceptable," Urbach said Friday.

Ten years after the fall of the Berlin Wall, much of the property in Poland that was confiscated by the Nazis, then nationalized by the communists, is no longer in Polish government hands. If the government still controls the property, the original owner would be registered as part owner on the deed.

Otherwise, according to the draft, owners would be compensated not in cash, but with Polish "reprivatization" bonds, which are valued at $8 billion.

Urbach decried the bonds, saying: "My people are not into the investment game. They are not looking to make a killing in the Polish stock market in the next 10 years." However, he said, "It is a great move in the right direction." Moshe Sanbar, the head of the Center of Organizations of Holocaust Survivors in Israel, gave qualified support to the draft legislation.

Preference must be given to those whose property was seized by the Nazis, Sanbar said. He wanted assurances in instances in which there are competing claims for the same property, from the Jewish owner whose property was confiscated by the Nazis, and from the post-war property-holder who lost it to the communists.

"Nazi activity must get the higher priority over communist confiscation," Sanbar said.

He also insisted that payments should be given to the heirs of the original owner, using the widest possible definition of heirs, and that heirs should be able to recover property regardless of where they currently live. Previously, Warsaw had said that property could be recovered by people living in Poland.

"If they don't give it to heirs, regardless of where they live now, the whole legislation is meaningless," Sanbar said.

The dominant focus of property restitution in the last

decade has been on the recovery of communal assets, including cemeteries, synagogues and schools in Central and Eastern Europe. Survivors in Israel and the US have grumbled that there has been insignificant attention paid to their efforts to recover their families' homes and businesses.

The Polish measure would cover the claims of those who were Polish citizens when the property was seized, including those whose property was in Polish territory that was later taken by the Soviet Union. However, it would exclude property that is in present-day Poland but was in Germany during the war.

In an effort to defend itself from lawsuits, Poland has argued that, as a sovereign state, it cannot be sued in American courts. However, in another property-related case filed in U.S. court in Chicago, a federal judge last month dismissed Poland's argument and ruled that it can be sued.

The property legislation was approved on Thursday by Prime Minister Jerzy Buzek's cabinet after more than 22 hours of debate, Deputy Treasury Minister Krzysztof Laszkiewicz announced on Friday. He said it provides a chance for progress on an issue of "unprecedented scope." He said that property seized by the communists that was later bought by private citizens in "good faith" will not be returned to original owners.

The measure still must be approved by the Polish parliament and President Aleksander Kwasniewski.

In addition to the claims of Holocaust survivors, there also are an anticipated 170,000 claims for farms and businesses seized by the post-war communist regime, which could total more than $27 billion, according to news accounts.

Sanbar, a retired banking executive, discounted Warsaw's concern that the restitution program could bankrupt the state.

"This is not necessarily a burden to the Polish government," he said. "If foreigners come and invest and develop those assets, it would assist the Polish economy."

In a related development, U.S. State Department mediator Henry Clarke is expected in Poland tomorrow to again try to break an acrimonious impasse between Polish Jews and the World Jewish Restitution Organization over a foundation that would control recovered communal property.

The meeting comes less than three months before Poland is scheduled to host an international conference on property restitution.

Stuart Eizenstat, the deputy Treasury secretary, complained earlier this summer that while the two sides argued over the composition of the foundation, the deadline for filing property claims was nearing.

The **Jerusalem Post** published the following article on September 17, 1999:

Polish Jews File Suit Against The Republic Of Poland

Two months ago, 11 victims of the Holocaust flied a class action law suit against the Polish government for the reprivatization of land seized during World War II. The lawsuit filed by attorneys Mel Urbach and Edward Klein in Federal court in Brooklyn, charged the Polish government and Treasury with illegally withholding victims' property from the survivors themselves or their heirs.

The allegations prompted an angry response from the Polish Foreign Ministry. "It's a rare example of linguistic aggression and disrespect for Polish history, which is used at the time when certain tangential points have emerged in Polish-Jewish dialogue," said spokesman Pawel Dobrowolski.

The Polish government has also responded with a number of defenses. They claim that the suit was brought in the wrong jurisdiction, that Poland has complete sovereignty and are net bound by the decisions of the courts in the

United States. The suit argues that Poland has been acting as a commercial real estate developer and not a sovereign nation with regards to confiscating and nationalizing Jewish owned property.

The government further claims that survivors willingly abandoned their property, thereby relinquishing their rights to it. However, the truth is that Jews were coerced into fleeing Poland by systematic violence and murder. Even after the war Urbach said many survivors returned to Poland to retake their property but were forced to leave. "Little was done by the Polish police and military to protect the Jews," when more than 1,000 Jews were murdered from 1945 to 1947.

According to restitution experts, almost every property claim can be documented in Poland because the record and deeds are well preserved in the archive. The names of the people who owned the property, as well as the dates that the property was bought are all recorded in detail. This makes Jewish claims to property easier to document than other countries.

The claim has got much attention in Poland by the media as well as the government. The case was on the front page of the Polish newspapers for several weeks. The 50-page legal brief was translated and printed word for word in the nationally syndicated papers. Many articles expressed their outrage for the claim saying that Poland is being blamed for the crimes of the Nazis. The articles further said that they had no knowledge of pogroms against Jews in post-war Poland. And even if true. Poland should not be blamed for the misdeeds of a few.

There is one group of Poles that has openly come out in favor of the lawsuit. The Polish Union of Property Owners (PUWN), which represents thousands of Poles who had their property seized under the Communist regime, has been trying unsuccessfully for years to obtain restitution through courts in Poland. Miraslow Shapowisky, the president of the organization, said that they might join the lawsuit in order to put further pressure on the government.

Due to the immense pressure that this case has generated, the Polish Parliament (SEJM) opened discussions on a proposed legislation package worth $15 billion to compensate survivors for their seized property. The bill would apply to all Polish victims or their heirs, whether Jewish or non-Jewish. The only limitation would be that the claimant was a Polish citizen at the time of the seizing.

If passed the bill would equip claimants with a way to regain their property if in government possession. If the land has been sold, it would provide for up to 60 percent of the real estate value, payable in government bonds which can be used to buy shares in lucrative government-backed industries.

Mr. Urbach said that he was very encouraged by the action in the Polish Parliament. Although there has been claim from the Poles that the lawsuit is meant to bankrupt the country. Mr. Urbach has said that this is not the case and that he will work with the government to come up with a reasonable settlement. He believes that "this piece of legislation will fold into a landmark settlement in the near future."

The United States government has been keeping a close eye on both the bill and lawsuit because of the tremendous repercussions it could have on the Polish economy. In fact, the Senate is considering holding hearings on the subject of Polish governments vast real estate holdings of which a tremendous amount are being claimed by Jewish survivors and heirs.

Meanwhile. Mr. Urbach will ask the European Union to also hold a fact-finding hearing in the fall on property restitution in Poland. The hearings would include testimony by survivors to relate post-war events in Poland. The hearings would be similar to those held by the U S. Senate last year about German slave labor.

As the pressure continues to mount on Poland, one can only wonder if after 55 years will there finally be justice. Ironically, Poland in December will host an international conference on the restitution of Jewish communal property.

Following is a news release from Congressman Anthony D. Weiner:

WEINER URGES POLISH GOVERNMENT TO RE-PATRIATE HOLOCAUST CLAIMS; 57 MEMBERS OF CONGRESS JOIN NEW YORK REP. IN CALL-ING FOR RESTITUTION
Washington DC–Congressman Anthony D. Weiner (D/1–Brooklyn & Queens), was joined today by Representative Henry A. Waxman (D-Ca) and 56 of their colleagues in the House of Representatives in a call for the Polish Government to pass comprehensive legislation to return assets seized by the Nazis and nationalized by the Communist government.

In a letter to Maciej Plazynski, Marshall of the Polish Sejm, the Polish Parliament, Congressman Weiner and his colleagues asked that the Sejm finally pass a comprehensive restitution law that would return 100% of all property and assets seized during the Holocaust and Communist eras to their rightful owners. The letter also commends Poland for its progress and leadership in repatriating communal property, but expresses concern that Poland has postponed a conference it pledged to hold on this issue in November 1999.

During World War II, the Nazi government occupying Poland seized the property of thousands of Jews and other persecuted peoples, evicting them from their homes, farms, factories and other real estate throughout Poland. After World War II, the communist government of Poland continued

these egregious practices by nationalizing assets and reject-
ing the claims of Holocaust survivors who sought repara-
tions.

In 1989, when the communist government was over-
thrown and the Republic of Poland was created, the new
Government announced its intent to compensate those who
had their property seized by former governments of Poland.
In the ten years since the fall of the Communist regime,
however, the Sejm has never seriously deliberated or voted
upon any of the re-privatization proposals that have been
introduced. As a result, thousands of Americans who were
Polish citizens at the time their property was expropriated
have been unable to seek restitution.

It is estimated that there are currently over 170,000
properties held in Poland that were wrongfully seized from
victims of the Holocaust and Communist terror. These properties have an estimated value of $20-$50 billion U.S. Dollars.

"There are currently thousands of former Polish citizens now in the United States who are seeking restitution
for their persecution by the Nazi and Communist regimes
in Poland," Weiner wrote to Marshal Plazynski. "As the people
involved are getting older and older every day, time is running out to compensate those wronged by the forced natu-
ralization of property. We urge you to work with your colleagues to accelerate the re-privatization effort, to ensure
that survivors of the Holocaust and Communist eras receive
the restitution they deserve."

Following is a news release issued by the New York City Council
on November 24, 1999:

**Dear Leads NYC Council in Call to Polish Government to
Make Restitution to Victims of Holocaust Era Property
Seizure**

The New York City Council (November 24, 1999) unanimously adopted a resolution calling upon the Republic of Poland to pass comprehensive legislation providing for the complete restitution of assets seized by the Nazis and nationalized by the Communist Polish government during and after the Holocaust. The resolution, authored by Council Member Moach Dear (D—Brooklyn), comes just days before the fairness hearing in the Swiss banks' $1.25 billion settlement of Holocaust victim claims.

The resolution notes that the democratic government in Poland has been in place since the fall of communism ten years ago. Yet, to date there has been no substantive legislative initiative to rectify the financial wrongs of its predecessor governments. The Nazis regularly appropriated the property of Holocaust victims. After World War II, the Communist government in Poland nationalized this stolen property. At the same time, the Communist government conducted a systematic campaign of persecution aimed at coercing its remaining Jewish population to flee. The private property belonging to these people was also nationalized. Efforts to provide for restitution to survivors and their descendents have not found significant support in the Sejm, the Polish legislature.

"It's time for the Polish Government to face its responsibility and return the stolen property of Holocaust survivors. Justice must be served as soon as possible so that the remaining survivors will see their property returned in their lifetimes," Dear emphasized. "It has been more than half a century since these egregious practices took place and more than ten years has passed since a democratically elected government was installed. I anxiously await a sincere effort to make restitution to the victims."

On January 9, 2000, the following article appeared in the *Jerusalem Post:*

New Polish law would bar Holocaust survivors from claiming property

By Marllyn Henry

NEW YORK (January 9, 2000)—Virtually all Holocaust survivors would effectively be barred from claiming family property in Poland under "anti-Jewish" amendments to a proposed Polish law intended to restore private property to victims of Nazi and communist confiscations, according to a victims' advocacy group in Warsaw.

The amendments to the government's reprivatization measure would limit claims to Polish citizens who lived in the country for at least five years before the legislation, said Kacper Krasicki of the Polish Union of Former Property Owners, which represents thousands of victims, primarily non-Jews.

"This would exclude all Jews from restitution, practically in one swoop," said New York attorney Mel Urbach, who last June filed a class-action suit against Poland to recover property that was confiscated or otherwise lost in World War II.

The exclusion is not limited to Jews, but also could affect tens of thousands of Poles who emigrated to the West.

The property legislation proposed by the government would have included all those who were Polish citizens when they lost property, and their descendants.

In addition to the claims of Holocaust survivors, there also are an anticipated 170,000 claims for farms and businesses seized by the post-war communist regime, which could total more than $27 billion.

Even before the parliamentary amendments, the government proposal had been attacked because it would restore only half of the value of the property.

It also would exclude property that is in present-day Poland but was in Germany during the war, leaving the

Jews of what was once the Silesian region of Breslau, and is now Wroclaw, without the possibility of recovery.

The amendments were passed unanimously by a parliamentary committee late last month, in what Krasicki called "an anti-Jewish step."

"The unanimous vote consists of proof of the true intention of Polish political leaders," he said. "They want to exclude totally the former Jewish holders from the benefits of the eventual bill."

Following is the amended class-action lawsuit filed March 8, 2000:

UNITED STATES DISTRICT COURT
EASTERN DISTRICT OF NEW YORK

THEO GARB, BELLA JUNGEWIRTH, SAM LEFKOWITZ, PETER KOPPENHEIM, JUDAH WELLER, CHANA LEWKOWICZ, SAMUEL GOLDIN, KARL DIAMOND, HALA SOBOL, GOLDIE KNOBEL, DAN LIPMAN, and WILLIAM Z. ZIMMERSPTIZ, Individually and on Behalf of Themselves and All Others Similarly Situated,
    Plaintiffs,

-against-
REPUBLIC OF POLAND and MINISTRY OF THE TREASURY OF POLAND (MINISTERSTWO SKARBU PANSTWA),
    Defendants.
CV-99-3487 (ERK) (MG)
AMENDED COMPLAINT

Plaintiffs, individually and on behalf of themselves and all others similarly situated, by their undersigned attorneys, as and for their Amended Complaint allege as follows:

OVERVIEW OF THE CLAIMS

1. This is a class action brought by twelve individual plaintiffs, on behalf of themselves and all others similarly situated, pursuant to 28 U.S.C. §§ 1330 *et seq.* and §§ 1602 *et seq.* (the "Foreign Sovereign Immunities Act") and other federal and state statutory and common laws and the law of nations against the Republic of Poland, hereinafter referred to at times as "Poland," and the Ministry of the Treasury of Poland ("Ministerstwo Skarb Panstwa"), hereinafter at times referred to as the "Treasury" or "Skarb."

2. Plaintiffs and the Class are Jewish owners of real properties and improvements thereon in Poland ("Property") during any part of the period from September 1, 1939 to May 30, 1945 and their heirs and successors. As a result of the Holocaust, the vast majority of Polish Jews were killed and their Property fell into the hands of the Nazis or their agents. Those who survived were forced to leave the country under emergency conditions.

3. Following World War II, Defendants engaged in a course of action designed to prevent surviving Polish Jews from asserting ownership interest over such Property by, among other things, participating in and fomenting anti-Semitic pogroms, failing to protect Jews returning to Poland, encouraging Jewish emigration from Poland, and adopting practices and procedures designed to frustrate inquiries by Class members regarding their Properties. Defendants then proceeded to exercise ownership or management rights over such Property, which they declared to be "abandoned" when they, in fact, knew or should have known that the owners or their heirs were alive, and profit from its ownership, management, or sale. Plaintiffs and the Class seek damages and other relief from Defendants for this ongoing conduct, which is in violation of international law and common law.

JURISDICTION AND VENUE

4. This Court has jurisdiction pursuant to section 1330 of the United States Judicial Code, 28 U.S.C. § 1330, as this action is against a foreign state, and section 1605(a) of the United States Judicial Code, 28 U.S.C. § 1605(a), as an exception to immunity under the Foreign Sovereign Immunities Act.

5. Venue is proper in this Court pursuant to 28 U.S.C. § 1391.

6. This Court has jurisdiction over the subject matter of this action pursuant to section 1605 of the Foreign Sovereign Immunities Act as follows:

(a) This action is based upon acts outside the territory of the United States in connection with commercial activities of a foreign state elsewhere, which acts cause a direct effect in the United States, under section 1605(a)(2); and

(b) This case is one in which rights in Properties taken in violation of international law are in issue and that Properties or any properties exchanged for such Properties is owned or operated by an agency or instrumentality of a foreign state and that agency or instrumentality is engaged in commercial activities in the United States, under section 1605(a)(3).

7. The transactions and ownership of Properties were and continue to be of the same type of activities commonly engaged in by private persons and entities. In addition, Defendants derived substantial profits in a wholly-commercial manner from real estate transactions related to Properties owned by Plaintiffs and the other members of the Class.

8. In regard to the allegations set forth herein, Poland and Skarb have engaged in commercial activities that are typically conducted by the private sector. A significant percentage of their operations involve the management, renting, leasing, and development of parcels of real property

and other valuable assets and the marketing and selling of such properties in and to persons located in the United States. These Properties were confiscated illegally from Jews living in Poland before, during, or after World War II through a calculated common scheme of anti-Semitism, undertaken or sanctioned by Poland in violation of international law, which culminated in the death, injury, maiming, and expulsion of thousands of Jews from Poland after the Holocaust, instilling in members of the Class a well-founded fear that Jews as a group would be persecuted in Poland because of their religion and membership in a distinct ethnic group should they return to that country.

9. Defendants have marketed and offered for sale to persons in the United States Properties that Defendants have improperly taken as provided herein.

10. Defendants have sold to persons in the United States Properties that Defendants have improperly taken as provided herein.

11. Defendants have used financial institutions in the United States to maintain Properties that Defendants have improperly taken as provided herein.

12. In sale transactions involving some Properties that Defendants have improperly taken as provided herein, Defendants have received money from United States financial institutions or from other financial institutions with offices in the United States.

13. Additionally, upon information and belief, all Defendants' reserves in the United States have been augmented and enhanced by profits earned by the illegal transactions in which they engaged, as described above.

14. Defendants have also engaged in other commercial activities within the United States and have raised capital through access to financial markets and financial institutions in the United States.

15. For a period of over fifty years, Poland and Skarb

fraudulently concealed the nature and extent of their involvement in transactions involving such looted Properties. Until recently, when previously secret documents have become accessible in Polish archives, Plaintiffs and the other Class members were unaware of the extent of Poland's and Skarb's fraudulent acts and conduct, and, thus, their right to a remedy against Poland and Skarb. In addition, Plaintiffs and the other members of the Class have, as a result of Defendants' conduct, suffered from fear to their safety should they take steps to enforce their rights in Poland so that Defendants' conduct deterred Plaintiffs and the other members of the Class from learning of the true condition of their Property and from enforcing such rights as they might have had with respect thereto. Consequently, Plaintiffs and the other Class members are entitled to the benefit of equitable tolling with respect to any limitations period.

PARTIES

PLAINTIFFS

16. *Theo Garb* ("Mr. Garb") is a U.S. citizen and resident of Long Island, New York. His late mother, Ruchla Rosenstrauch-Garbarz, shared ownership with her siblings of the building at 45 Targowa Street, a large apartment building in the Praga district of Warsaw. Until the onset of World War II she received commercial income from that ownership. Upon information and belief, none of Ruchla Rosenstrauch-Garbarz's siblings or or their heirs survived the Holocaust.

17. Ruchla Rosenstrauch-Garbarz has since died, and Mr. Garb is her sole heir. At the time of her death, Ruchla Rosenstrauch-Garbarz had not transferred her ownership interest in any portion of 45 Targowa Street nor had that ownership interest been transferred from her except by reason of the wrongful conduct of Defendants as alleged herein.

18. Since his mother's death, Mr. Garb has undertaken to recover the Properties at 45 Targowa Street without suc-

cess. Among other things, he traveled to Poland where he was granted access only to old ledgers but denied access to more recent documents, which would show in whose name title to the Properties at 45 Targowa Street is held. The building is believed to be fully rented, with commercial stores on the ground floor. Neither Mr. Garb nor any other member of his family has ever received any compensation for the unlawful taking of his family's Property.

19. ***Bella Jungewirth (née Neustadt)*** ("Mrs. Jungewirth") is a native of Poland who is a U.S. citizen and lives in New York, New York. Before World War II, she lived in a building owned by her parents in Krakow, Poland. Of her immediate family—which consisted of both of her parents and six siblings—only she survived World War II and death at the hands of the Nazis.

20. Having survived Auschwitz, she returned to Krakow in 1945 to take possession of her parents' house. At that time it was occupied by a Polish woman who said that she paid rent to the Treasury. Mrs. Jungewirth was threatened with death by the occupants of her home if she tried to regain possession of her Property. After having received multiple death threats, Mrs. Jungewirth fled Poland shortly thereafter.

21. Mrs. Jungewirth's efforts to reclaim her Property have proved unsuccessful, __en though records recently uncovered in Polish archives confirm that her family owned the Property. Based on information and belief, following the Holocaust, Skarb registered itself as the "owner" of the Property, managed the Property, and sold it in 1957, without providing Mrs. Jungewirth with any notice or opportunity to reclaim it or giving her any compensation for the taking.

22. ***Sam Lefkowitz*** ("Mr. Lefkowitz") was also born in Poland. He is a U.S. citizen and lives in Florida. His father, Jacob Lefkowitz, owned a large leather export business and

several parcels of real estate, including a thirty-two family residence located at 9 Ulica Warshawska, in Czestochowa, Poland.

23. Mr. Lefkowitz escaped from the Treblinka concentration camp and hid in a stable until he was liberated by Soviet troops in late 1944. Upon his return to Czestochowa, he discovered that the 9 Ulica Warshawska Property was being controlled by its former superintendent. After learning that other Jewish survivors were attacked in Czestochowa, some seriously, and receiving several threats himself, Mr. Lefkowitz fled Poland.

24. Mr. Lefkowitz is the heir to his father's estate, including the Property at 9 Ulica Warshawska, but he has been unable to pursue his recovery of that Property in Poland.

25. _Peter Koppenheim_ ("Mr. Koppenheim") is a British citizen and lives in Manchester, England. He was born in a Bresslau, which is in a part of Germany that became part of Poland after World War II. His grandfather Meyer Koppenheim owned a five story house on Ring 7, in Bresslau, as well as several other buildings in the same city.

26. In 1939, the Koppenheim house was seized by the Nazis and purchased by a Nazi sympathizer.

27. After World War II, when Bresslau became part of Poland, all German assets there came under the control of Skarb or other instrumentalities of Poland. Mr. Koppenheim retained lawyers in Germany in the 1990's, but, over his objection, Skarb and Poland permitted the grandchildren of the Nazi sympathizer who was permitted to "purchase" that Property from the occupying Nazis, to sell it to the Thyssen Companies, part of the Krupp Group, for several million Deutsch Marks. Mr. Koppenheim has not received any compensation for the Property notwithstanding that he was its rightful owner at the time of the sale.

28. *Judah Weller* ("Mr. Weller") is a U.S. citizen and resides in Queens, New York. His father, Sruel Eizik Weller, was a Polish national who avoided the Holocaust by fleeing to Brazil before September 1939. His family was to follow, but was trapped by the German invasion in September 1939 and killed in 1942. The family owned and ran a store at 8 Warsaw Street, Kaluszyn, Poland, which has been taken from the family and never returned. Sruel Eizik Weller left Brazil, became a U.S. citizen, remarried and raised a new family. He died in 1973.

29. In 1999, Mr. Weller initiated an investigation into the Property in Kaluszyn. Eventually, records were uncovered showing that Mr. Weller's father's first wife purportedly sold the Property in 1950, eight years *after* she was murdered by the Nazis. At that time, Defendants knew that the first Mrs. Weller had been killed in 1942.

30. Mr. Weller has not received any compensation for his family's Property in Poland, to which he is entitled.

31. *Chana Lewkowicz* ("Ms. Lewkowicz") is a U.S. citizen living in Brooklyn, New York. Her parents owned a parcel of Property on Rynek Glowny 14 in the city of Oswiecim, Poland, more commonly known as Auschwitz. During the Nazi occupation of Poland, her parents were evicted from the house and the Nazis turned it into a court. During World War II, Ms. Lewkowicz was sent to various concentration camps where she was forced to work as a slave laborer. After World War II, she returned to her home, whereupon she was threatened by its occupants. She fled, ironically, to Germany for her safety. The Polish Treasury took the Property and has refused to return it to Ms. Lewkowicz. The building is still used as a courthouse. To date, Ms. Lewkowicz has not received any compensation for this Property. Her parents also owned other Property, but she has been unable to find the pertinent records.

32. *Samuel Goldin* ("Mr. Goldin") was born in 1916 in Nieswiez, Poland and is a U.S. citizen living in Binghamton, New York.

33. His father, Mowsza Goldin, owned, with Jacob Sadowski, a Warsaw business named Tartak Radzyminski, which owned a large tract of land with railroad tracks for four rail cars, a large factory and an office building. Mowsza Goldin and Mr. Goldin's mother were killed at the Auschwitz concentration camp.

34. With his two sisters, both of whom also survived World War II, Mr. Goldin is the heir to his father's Property, including the interest in Tartak Radzyminski and, through it, the Warsaw realty. Since World War II he has tried, without success, to obtain title to that Property.

35. After World War II, Mr. Goldin learned from other Jewish survivors that the Nazis took control of his father's factory as soon as they entered Warsaw. The most recent property records he was able to obtain, from 1996, show that Skarb and the Polish Treasury are the "owners" of the factory and continue to run the business and receive income from it to the present day.

36. *Karl Diamond* ("Mr. Diamond") was born and raised in Tarnow, Poland, and is a U.S. citizen residing in Memphis, Tennessee. Before World War II, Mr. Diamond's family owned a pickling business and a store as well as a vast forest, which was lumbered once a year. The forest land was owned by Mr. Diamond's father and uncle, and consisted of approximately 240 acres in Stempina near Frystak (Powiat Strzyzow), Poland.

37. On June 12, 1942, Mr. Diamond's family, along with the other Jewish inhabitants of Tarnow, were evicted under the pretext of "resettlement" by the Nazis. Mr. Diamond was sent to the Plaszow slave labor camp, where he remained until he was liberated by Soviet troops in 1945.

38. After World War II, Mr. Diamond retained lawyers in Poland and Israel seeking to recover his family's Property. He learned that his father's real estate was taken by Skarb after World War II, but has been unable to reclaim any of it. Defendants have resisted his ongoing efforts to recover his family's Property.

39. *Hala Sobol* ("Ms. Sobol") was born in Poland in 1924 and is a U.S. citizen and resident of Ohio. Her uncle Mottel Horn owned a large building on a property fronting on two main streets in downtown Krakow, Poland; one side of the Property is located on ul. Bozego Ciala 23 and the other side on ul. Krakowska 26. He died at the Auschwitz concentration camp.

40. Mottel Horn's Krakow Property was confiscated and subdivided after World War II, with a bank registered as its "owner." Ms. Sobol is the sole heir with respect to that Property.

41. In addition, Mottel Horn purchased a villa in Rabka, ul. Poniatowskiego 185, Poland in 1930.

42. Ms. Sobol's grandparents owned two houses in Kshanow, ul. Malarinik 3, which are no longer standing, having been demolished by Skarb.

43. Ms. Sobol's aunt and uncle, who owned several of the family's properties, are deceased and had no children. All of Ms. Sobol's other relatives in the family were murdered during the Holocaust, leaving Ms. Sobol and her sister as the only survivors of her entire family. Ms. Sobol's sister died three years ago, and is survived by one daughter in London.

44. Ms. Sobol was liberated by the British army at the Bergen Belsen concentration camp. Her physical and mental condition was extremely poor after the liberation–having spent five years under Nazi occupation. She wanted to return to Poland to reclaim her family's Property, but was warned of the dangerous situation and the wave of anti-Semitism

that was being unleashed against the returning Jewish survivors. She then fled the country. Ms. Sobol and her family have not received any compensation for the Property that was confiscated by Defendants.

45. *Goldie Knobel* ("Ms. Knobel") was born on July 9, 1942 in Dukla, Poland. She is a U.S. citizen and lives in Brooklyn, New York. Her mother, Yochwet Knobel (née Feit), owned and managed two large international convalescent hotels and spas in Ivonitch, Poland, in partnership with her brother, Nochum Feit. They also owned Ivonitch-Edtrov private houses in which they lived.

46. Shortly after the invasion of Poland in 1939, the Nazis ordered the entire Knobel family to evacuate the Ivonitch buildings, which they did. The family remained in hiding for the next five years.

47. After World War II, the Knobel family emerged from hiding and was directed to go to Stetin, Poland, where they were registered. They were later sent to a displaced persons ("DP") camp in Berlin, and in 1951 came to the United States from there.

48. Nochum Feit also returned to Stetin, Poland, with the Knobel family. He had been in hiding with the Knobel family. One day in 1946, he went out to visit a government office and failed to return. Sometime later he was found dead, hacked to death with a sharp weapon by local Poles. When trying to report the death, they were forced to flee for their lives.

49. The Knobel family had been threatened by Poles before the murder. They had been told that if they tried to remain in Poland, they would all be killed. After the brutal death of Nochum, they felt compelled to flee Poland, going to a displaced persons camp.

50. Ms. Knobel's parents lived the rest of their lives in Brooklyn, New York. Her father died in the 1980's and her

mother died in the 1990's. While alive, both of Ms. Knobel's parents were terrified of ever returning to Poland.

51. Ms. Knobel seeks the return of the real Property that belonged to her family before World War II, to which she is the rightful heir.

52. *Dan Lipman* ("Mr. Lipman") was born in 1919 in Lodz, Poland. His given name is Lipman Yedidyah Lipmanowicz. His father was Kiva Lipmanowicz and his mother was Jura Lipmanowicz Kleinlerer, a daughter of Moses Kleinlerer. He currently lives in Chicago, Illinois.

53. Mr. Lipman left Poland in 1940, and is the sole survivor of his family.

54. Before World War II, his mother's family owned several Properties in Lodz, Poland, at 38 Jaracza Street (formerly 38 Cegielniana), 8 Plac Wolnosci (formerly 4 Plac Koscielny), and 8 Pilsudskiego. Title to each of these Properties is currently held by either Poland or an instrumentality of the City of Lodz.

55. Mr. Lipman is the sole heir to his family's Property, including the real Properties in Lodz.

56. Mr. Lipman, a representative of the Sub-Class as well as the Class, seeks the return of the real Property that belonged to his family before World War II, to which he is the rightful heir.

57. *William Z. Zimmersptiz* ("Mr. Zimmerspitz") was born on May 8, 1926 in Krokow, Poland. He currently lives in Cherry Hill, New Jersey.

58. Before World War II, his parents owned a twelve unit apartment house at 4 Podskale, Krakow, Poland. His father, Szymon Zimmerspitz, died in a concentration camp in or about 1944. His mother, Rozalia Zimmerspitz, died after World War II. When Mr. Zimmerspitz married in 1953, Rozalia Zimmerspitz gave all of her interest in the Properties in Krakow to Mr. Zimmerspitz.

59. Before World War II, Mr. Zimmerspitz's maternal

grandparents, Szmerl and Tauba Gemiiner, owned a 20 unit apartment house at 61 Dietlowska, Krakow, Poland. Both of these grandparents were killed by the Germans in 1943.

60. Titles to the Properties at 4 Podskale and 61 Dietlowska, Krakow are currently believed to be held by Poland or Skarb.

61. Mr. Zimmerspitz is the sole heir to his family's Property, including the real Properties in Krakow.

62. Mr. Zimmerspitz, a representative of the Sub-Class as well as the Class, seeks the return of the real Property that belonged to his family before World War II, to which he is the rightful heir.

DEFENDANTS

63. Republic of Poland and Skarb, through their ministers, officers and directors, conduct the affairs of Poland.

64. Upon information and belief, Poland and Skarb do business in the United States. A portion of all of Defendants' financial activities are directed at, and impact upon, persons in the United States. At all relevant times, Defendants have maintained substantial quantities of assets in the United States, including New York, and/or have places of business in the United States or continuously and systematically transact business in the United States.

65. Defendants have committed tortious acts outside the United States which acts have caused injury to persons within the United States, and Defendants regularly do or solicit business and engage in a persistent course of conduct within the state.

66. After World War II, Defendants coordinated and participated in a scheme to force Jewish Holocaust survivors to flee from Poland, through the use and threat of violence, culminating in the death, injury, and maiming of thousands of Jews from Poland, in violation of the laws of nations.

67. Defendants have committed tortious acts outside the United States which acts have caused injury to persons within the United States, and Defendants expect or should reasonably expect those acts to have consequences in the United States, and Defendants derive substantial revenue from international commerce.

CLASS ALLEGATIONS

68. Plaintiffs seek to represent a Class comprised of the following:

a. All Jewish persons and entities (and their heirs and successors) who owned real property and improvements thereon in Poland during the period September 1, 1939 to May 30, 1945 as to which Defendants exercised any rights of ownership or management and who have not been compensated.

69. Fed. *R. Civ. P. 23(a)(1).* The proposed Class is so numerous that individual joinder of all its members is impracticable under the standards of Fed. R. Civ. P. 23(a)(1). Thousands of persons are members of the Class, residing throughout the United States and elsewhere. While the exact number and identities of the Class members are unknown at this time, such information can be ascertained through appropriate investigation and discovery.

70. Fed. *R. Civ. P. 23(a)(2) and 23(b)(3).* There are questions of law and fact that are common with respect to all members of the Class and that predominate over any individual issues that may exist. Common questions of fact and law include the following:

i. Whether Defendants conducted or participated in a scheme of threats, violence, beatings, murder, expulsions and racial cleansing against the Jews of Poland in the post-World War II period in Poland.

ii. Whether Defendants engaged in a course of conduct to illegally seize, confiscate, or benefit from the Properties of Class members and commercially control, manage and alienate such Properties in violation of the rights and entitlements of Class members.

iii. Whether Defendants obtained profits through their transactions in Properties taken from Class members.

iv. Whether Defendants knowingly or intentionally concealed their participation in transactions involving such looted Properties.

v. Whether Defendants, after they understood that they had dealt in, held and profited from transactions involving such looted Properties, refused to disgorge such Properties and the profits unjustly earned therefrom to their rightful owners.

71. Fed. R. Civ. P. 23(a)(3). Plaintiffs' claims are typical of the claims of the other members of the Class. Plaintiffs and all other members of the Class have been similarly affected and harmed by Defendants' course of conduct.

72. Fed. R. _Civ. P. 23(a)(4)._ The Class representatives will fairly and adequately protect the interests of the members of the Class, and do not have interests which are antagonistic to the interests of other Class members. The Class representatives have retained attorneys experienced in the prosecution of complex litigation and class action litigation.

73. _Fed. R. Civ. P. 23(b)(3)._ A class action is superior to other available methods for the fair, efficient and just adjudication of this litigation. Individual joinder of all members of the Class is impractical. Even if individual Class members had the resources to pursue individual litigation, it would be unduly burdensome to the courts in which the individual litigation would proceed. The class action device allows a single court to provide the benefits of unitary adjudication, judicial economy, and the fair and equitable handling of all plaintiffs' claims in a single forum. The prosecution of this action as a class action conserves the resources of the parties and of the judicial system, and protects the rights of each Class member. Furthermore, for many, if not most,

Class members, a class action is the only feasible mechanism that allows them an opportunity for legal redress and justice.

SUB-CLASS ALLEGATIONS

74. Plaintiffs Dan Lippman and William Zimmerspitz (the "Sub-Class Representatives") also seek to represent a Sub-Class comprised of the following:

Members of the Class defined in paragraph hereof whose Property is currently held by either Defendant or by an instrumentality of the Polish government or any other political sub-division of Poland.

75. _Fed. R. Civ. P. 23(a)(1)._ The proposed Sub-Class is so numerous that individual joinder of all its members is impracticable under the standards of Fed. R. Civ. P. 23(a)(1). Thousands of persons are members of the Sub-Class. While the exact number and identities of the Sub-Class members are unknown at this time, such information can be ascertained through appropriate investigation and discovery.

76. _Fed. R. Civ. P. 23(a)(2) and 23(b)(3)._ There are questions of law and fact that are common with respect to all members of the Sub-Class and that predominate over any individual issues that may exist. These questions include those generally applicable to the Class, set forth at Paragraph , but also include the following:

i.   Whether Defendants or any other instrumentality of the Polish government or any political sub-division of Poland holds title to Property that is rightfully owned by members of the Sub-Class;

ii.   Whether transfers of Property from either Defendant to any other instrumentality of the Polish government or any political sub-division of Poland was done without adequate consideration and was otherwise sham transactions so that such instrumentalities of the Polish government or political sub-divisions of Poland were with respect to such "transfers" actually alter egos of Defendants for which

Defendants bear responsibility with respect to such Property.

77. *Fed. R. Civ. P. 23(a)(3).* Plaintiffs' claims are typical of the claims of the other members of the Sub-Class. Plaintiffs and all other members of the Sub-Class have been similarly affected and harmed by Defendants.

78. *Fed. R. Civ. P. 23(a)(4).* The Sub-Class Representatives will fairly and adequately protect the interests of the members of the Sub-Class, and do not have interests which are antagonistic to the interests of other Sub-Class members. The Sub-Class Representatives have retained attorneys experienced in the prosecution of complex litigation and class action litigation.

79. *Fed. R. Civ. P. 23(b)(3).* A class action is superior to other available methods for the fair, efficient and just adjudication of this litigation. Individual joinder of all members of the Sub-Class is impractical. Even if individual Sub-Class members had the resources to pursue individual litigation, it would be unduly burdensome to the courts in which the individual litigation would proceed. Individual litigation magnifies the delay and expense to all parties in the court system of resolving the controversies engendered by Defendants' conduct. The class action device allows a single court to provide the benefits of unitary adjudication, judicial economy, and the fair and equitable handling of all plaintiffs' claims in a single forum. The prosecution of this action as a class action conserves the resources of the parties and of the judicial system, and protects the rights of each Sub-Class member. Furthermore, for many, if not most, Sub-Class members, a class action is the only feasible mechanism that allows them an opportunity for legal redress and justice.

FACTS

80. On the eve of the Holocaust, there were over three million Jews living in Poland, representing about one in ten

Poles. This was the largest single concentration of Jewish population, representing one in five of the world's Jews.

81. In Eastern Europe, including Poland, Jewish life centered around major cities. In Warsaw, approximately thirty-three percent of the population was Jewish. In Krakow, it was approximately twenty-five percent; in Lodz, approximately thirty-four percent; in Kielce, half of the population was Jewish.

82. The Jews in Poland in the years immediately preceding the Holocaust paid approximately thirty percent of the taxes collected by the Polish government.

83. On September 1, 1939, the armed forces of Nazi Germany invaded Poland from the west. Pursuant to a previously arranged plan, Soviet armed forces advanced into eastern Poland. After Polish armed resistance was quelled, Germany and the Soviet Union divided Poland between themselves. Germany eventually attacked its former ally and occupied all of pre-war Poland. The Nazis used Polish soil as the principal ground for their plan to kill the Jews of Europe.

84. As an integral part of the Nazi master plan to achieve a "final solution of ethnic cleansing" and as a component of their strategy to dominate Europe and beyond, the Nazis set about looting the assets of the very peoples they sought to liquidate. The group that suffered the most from these policies was European Jews. Mass extermination was preceded, accompanied, and followed by a methodical, systematic, and industrialized confiscation of Properties, including through the enactment of illegal statutes, forcible-taking of property, extortion, blackmail, and murder.

85. Billions of dollars worth of Property owned by Jews in Poland were misappropriated by the Nazis. Individual Jewish businesses were put under the administration of Nazi-controlled "treuhandlers," who controlled all the

assets of the Jewish-owned companies and used such Properties for the benefit of their Nazi masters.

86. Before and during the early months of Nazi occupation, a small percentage of Polish Jews escaped to the West
or Palestine. Many others fled the Nazi terror by moving
eastward to the area controlled by the Soviet Union and
later, when hostilities began between that country and Germany, into Russia itself. By the end of the war, over 250,000
Polish Jews had found temporary refuge in Soviet territory.

87. As Soviet troops began to move westward into
Germany, the issue of the resettlement of Polish Jews then in
Russia was the subject of considerable diplomatic discus-
sion. At the conference at Yalta in February 1945, the Allies
agreed that the borders of post-War Europe would be
changed. Poland would be reconfigured westward, acquir-
ing a large portion of former German territory to the west,
but losing a similar portion of its eastern territory to the
Soviet Union. The borders of Ukraine, Belorussia, Russia,
and Lithuania were also to be changed from their pre-War
locations.

88. The Allies recognized that these modified borders
would result in significant ethnic minorities in these countries. Consequently, it was agreed that Poles, Ukrainians,
Belorussians, Russians, and Lithuanians could relocate within
the new borders of their homelands. The principal opposi-
tion to this agreement came from the Polish exile leader,
Wladislaw Gomulka, who was to become Poland's post-War
Communist dictator. Gomulka's strongly held belief was
that Poland should become a single nationality state. This
left no room for Jews, who Gomulka viewed as being inher-
ently non-Polish. Under extreme pressure from Stalin, who
did not want a large population of Polish Jews left in Russia,
Gomulka reluctantly consented to allow Polish, Jewish refugees to return.

89. At the end of World War II, the only Jews remaining in Poland were those who were freed from the concentration camps—most of the survivors of the camps were non-Jews—who were largely non-Polish, those fighting with partisan units, and those few who had successfully evaded the Nazis. The millions of Polish Jews who had fled or had been murdered had left behind a huge inventory of abandoned properties. By the end of the War, many of those properties not destroyed had been taken over by non-Jewish Poles.

90. On July 6, 1945, the Soviet Union and Poland entered into a repatriation agreement which resulted in the return of about 230,000, or 90%, of the Polish Jews who had fled to the Soviet Union. At the same time, Poland was receiving a huge influx from the West of Poles who had been impressed into forced labor within Germany. The Polish Government, now under the leadership of Gomulka, saw this chaotic situation as a pretext to effectuate its plan to rid Poland of the Jews it never wanted to take back in the first place. It also played on the fears of the population that returning Jews would seek to reclaim their property.

91. A common scheme of savage, unchecked, anti-Semitism was unleashed against returning Jews, killing, maiming, and injuring thousands of defenseless returning Jewish Poles. The Polish government, people, police, and army were actual participants.

92. Polish governmental entities thus fanned the flames of anti-Semitism and when outbreaks occurred, stood by as Jews were victimized. In June 1945, forty Jews were killed within a space of ten days. On August 11 of that year, police and security service personnel participated in a pogrom in Krakow. There were no repercussions to any of the participants.

93. The governmental campaign to oust the Jews of Poland reached its peak in the pogrom of July 4, 1946 at Kielce. There, in broad daylight, a mob led by uniformed

police and security personnel attacked the building in which the local Jewish Committee was headquartered. Forty-two Jews were killed and about eighty were injured. In similar incidents throughout the country, thirty-three other Jews were murdered in July 1946. In none of these instances did Polish governmental officials either come to the aid of the Jews being attacked or take criminal action against the perpetrators, which included governmental officials.

94. Polish soldiers escorting wounded Jews to a nearby hospital beat and robbed their Jewish charges on the way. Polish soldiers directly participated in the murder of Jews and the looting of their Property. The head of the Provincial Bureau for Public Security, a Major Sobczynski, in charge of security in Kielce, has been directly implicated in escalating this pogrom.

95. The Kielce pogrom had the effect intended by the Polish Government. Fearful for their lives, Jews sought to flee Poland. Although strict immigration controls were applicable in Poland at the time, the Polish Government undercut its own laws in encouraging and tacitly allowing Jews to leave the country. By September 1946, 63,000 Jews had fled. Within a year, 180,000 Polish Jews were living in displaced persons camps outside of Poland. The property belonging to these Jews were declared to be abandoned.

96. After the post-War exodus, very few Jews were left in Poland. The Arab-Israeli conflicts of 1956 and 1967 provided further pretexts for the Polish Government to oppress the Jews remaining in Poland. In each instance, the Polish Government fomented and encouraged anti-Semitic riots and other actions. In 1967, some 9,000 Jews were dismissed from their jobs. Again, in fear of their lives and livelihoods, Jews chose to emigrate leaving behind properties and possessions.

The Role of Poland and Skarb

97. Before the Holocaust, middle and upper class Jews owned significant assets and properties in Poland. At the onset of the Holocaust, many Jews buried or hid whatever assets they could on their properties in order to avoid anticipated looting by the Nazis.

98. At the end of World War II and the Holocaust, survivors, many gravely ill from abuse and neglect suffered in German labor and concentration camps, returned to their homes in Poland, seeking their family members and possessions and hoping to resume their lives. Others, who had fled into the Soviet Union and elsewhere, also returned to their former homes in Poland after World War II.

99. The Polish administration and the local Poles did not welcome this return of Jews. Poles wrongfully took possession of Jewish Properties before Jewish survivors had returned, with no intention of restoring ownership, control, or management of such Properties to their rightful owners.

100. Polish Jews were not accepted back to Poland. As more fully described above, the Polish government undertook a campaign to bring an end to the 1,000 year Jewish presence there, and were not prepared to allow the Jews to resettle and regain ownership of their Properties and other assets. Instead, a horrific plan was put into action.

101. Many properties belonging to Jews in Poland had been initially confiscated by the Nazis. As the Nazis retreated, Jewish survivors tried unsuccessfully to return to the Properties. After forcing returning Jews out of Poland, Poland and Skarb seized these assets and treated them as their own, without any attempt to locate survivors and heirs who had ownership rights to those Properties.

102. Subsequently, the Polish Government passed a series of illegal, self-serving laws allowing for the change of title to it of "abandoned property," which was designed to and had the effect of providing "legitimacy" to the taking of

title to Jewish Property. In fact, because these "abandoned" Properties had not been abandoned but were unoccupied or unclaimed or otherwise "abandoned" by their true owners solely as a result of Defendants' improper conduct complained of herein. These laws could not legitimize the Property takings that were improper and illegal, including under the laws of nations.

103. Even in the post-Communist era, access to courts for Class members in order to establish their rights and interests in the Properties seized, or to recover damages for the value thereof, has been substantially denied, and there has been no statutory resolution to these issues.

104. Since the Holocaust, survivors and their heirs have tried to regain their Properties, mostly without any success.

105. Until recently, it has been impossible to gain access to the relevant documents to substantiate a property claim in Poland for Jewish survivors and their heirs. Even today, it is extremely difficult for Jews to gain the cooperation of Polish authorities that is necessary to pursue such claims.

106. As a result of the foregoing, Plaintiffs and the other members of the Class have suffered persecution because of their religion and membership in an ethnic group.

107. Because of threats, acts of violence and futility, members of the Class had and have a well-founded fear of future persecution which prevents them from returning to Poland or taking appropriate action to reclaim their Properties. These fears are justified and reasonable under the circumstances.

The Knowledge of Poland and Skarb

108. At all times relevant to the events described herein, ministers, officers, and directors of Poland and Skarb knew, or were in possession of such information that they should have known, that they were part of an improper and unlawful scheme that (i) resulted in depriving Jewish Holocaust

victims and their heirs of their Properties, and (ii) provided Poland and Skarb with enormous profits from the use and enjoyment of such Properties.

109. From 1945 and onward, Defendants were aware of the circumstances under which they were confiscating Jewish-owned Properties. They nonetheless continued to assume ownership rights over those Properties on a massive level and engaged in a course of conduct designed to result in the "abandonment" of Properties by Class members and the intimidation of Class members from asserting their ownership rights in such Properties.

110. Defendants have never attempted to determine which Property owners survived World War II. They have made no reasonable effort to locate living heirs. Defendants' conduct in orchestrating and participating in a scheme to coerce Jews to flee Poland under threat of death, torture, and physical injury was a violation of international law.

AS AND FOR A FIRST CLAIM FOR RELIEF
Violation of International Law

111. Plaintiffs repeat and reallege the allegations contained in paragraphs 1 through as if the same were fully set forth herein.

112. Poland and Skarb violated customary international law enforceable in this Court as federal common law and the law of nations, as exemplified by the Nuremberg Principles, the Hague Convention of 1907, the Polish Minority Treaty of 1919, and the Geneva Convention of 1929.

113. Defendants violated such customary international laws by creating, participating in, and/or failing to prevent acts to dispossess permanently an ethnic and religious group from their Properties and from Poland itself after the Holocaust and by trafficking in, managing, and commercially profiting from the Properties looted from Plaintiffs and the other Class members, and failing to disgorge, concealing and refusing to disgorge such assets and the profits obtained

from such assets, all of which were obtained pursuant to crimes against an ethnic and racial minority in an on-going scheme that has continued for the last fifty-five years.

114. Among other things, Defendants' conduct complained of herein constituted the practice, encouragement, or condoning, as a matter of state policy, genocide, degrading treatment or punishment against Jews, and systematic racial and religious discrimination.

115. By reason of the foregoing, Plaintiffs and the other members of the Class have been damaged in an amount to be determined at trial.

AS AND FOR A SECOND CLAIM FOR RELIEF
Conversion

116. Plaintiffs repeat and reallege the allegations contained in paragraphs 1 through as if the same were fully set forth herein.

117. Poland and Skarb have wrongfully converted, used, operated, managed and alienated Plaintiffs' and the other Class members' Properties for their own use and benefit, in violation of customary international laws.

118. By reason of the foregoing, Plaintiffs and the other members of the Class have been damaged in an amount to be determined at trial.

AS AND FOR A THIRD CLAIM FOR RELIEF
Constructive Trust

119. Plaintiffs repeat and reallege the allegations contained in paragraphs 1 through as if the same were fully set forth herein.

120. By reason of the foregoing, with respect to the income and profits generated before the trial of this Action from the Properties properly belonging to Plaintiffs and the other Class members, Plaintiffs and the other Class members are entitled to have Defendants declared to be constructive trustees and required to turn such income and profits over to Plaintiffs and the other members of the Class.

121. Such turnover of income and profits shall be in addition to the award of damages to Plaintiffs and the other members of the Class for the value of their Properties as of the time of the trial of this Action.

AS AND FOR A FOURTH CLAIM FOR RELIEF
Accounting

122. Plaintiffs repeat and reallege the allegations contained paragraphs 1 through as if the same were fully set forth herein.

123. Poland and Skarb fraudulently concealed the Properties converted from Plaintiffs and the other Class members, and have, for the last fifty-four years, concealed the profits obtained from such Properties, all of which were obtained as a direct result of the improper scheme alleged herein.

124. Defendants have consistently withheld and misrepresented information concerning the status and disposition of such Properties, and the profits realized therefrom, and have failed and refused to account for the same, such that Plaintiffs and the other Class members are entitled to an accounting as to the amount and disposition of all such Properties and profits.

AS AND FOR A FIFTH CLAIM FOR RELIEF
By Sub-Class, For Restitution

125. Plaintiffs repeat and reallege the allegations contained in paragraphs 1 through as if the same were fully set forth herein.

126. This claim is brought on behalf of a sub-class consisting of Class members whose Property is currently held by either Defendant or any other Polish governmental body or instrumentality.

127. Defendants and other Polish governmental bodies or instrumentalities purport to hold title to Property that was improperly taken from Class members as described herein.

128. As a result of the foregoing, such title is defective and subject to the superior rights of members of the Sub-Class.

129. As a result of the foregoing, each member of the Sub-Class is entitled to be restored in his title to the Property that was improperly taken by Defendants and for which either Defendants purport to have title.

130. With respect to a significant amount of real Property that was improperly taken by Defendants as alleged herein, official title has been transferred to the municipality or other local government, or an agency or instrumentality thereof, in which the Property is located. Such transfers have been for little or no consideration.

131. For example, the Property at 38 Jaracza Street, Lodz, to which Mr. Lippman is entitled, was transferred from Skarb (which had wrongly taken title) to the Lodz commune, a local governmental body, free of charge in 1992 pursuant to a 1990 Polish law that authorized such free transfers to local governments without consideration.

132. Such municipalities and other governmental entities are, with respect to such Property, the alter egos of Defendants.

133. As a result, insofar as a title to a piece of real Property that was, for the reasons set forth herein, improperly taken from a member of the Sub-Class is held by a municipality or other local government, or an agency or instrumentality thereof, in which the Property is located as a result of either Defendant transferring such title for little or no consideration, each member of the Sub-Class who is entitled to such Property is entitled to be restored in his title to such Property from the municipality or other governmental entity in whose name title is currently held.

134. With respect to the Sub-Class members whose title, as set forth herein, is superior to that of the Defendant or other Polish governmental body or instrument that

currently "holds" title, they are entitled to a declaration that they are the true title holder and to the return of that Property.

135. The members of this Sub-Class have no adequate remedy at law.

WHEREFORE, Plaintiffs, on behalf of themselves and all other Class members, pray that the Court:

i.   Certify a class comprised of members as identified in paragraph hereof and declare Plaintiffs' counsel to be counsel to the Class;

ii.   Certify a sub-class comprised of members as identified in paragraph hereof and declare Plaintiffs' counsel to be counsel to the sub-Class;

iii. Declare that Poland and Skarb, by their conduct complained of herein, violated international law with respect to Plaintiffs and the other members of the Class;

iv. Award damages to Plaintiffs and the other members of the Class from Poland and Skarb, jointly and severally, in an amount to be determined at the trial of this Action;

v. On the third claim for relief, declare that Poland and Skarb are constructive trustees of the all of Plaintiffs' and the other Class members' Properties, and the income and profits derived therefrom, held and realized by Defendants, and direct said Defendants to compensate Plaintiffs and the other Class members appropriately;

vi. On the fourth claim for relief, order an audit of Poland's and Skarb's transactions from 1945 to the present involving the Properties of Plaintiffs and the other Class members in Poland, and direct them to account to Plaintiffs and the other Class members for all such Properties, income and profits;

vii. On the fifth claim for relief, declaring each member of the Sub-Class to be the right and true owner of the Property to which he has true title and ordering the restitution of that Property to that sub-Class member;

viii. Award to Plaintiffs and the Class the costs and expenses of this action, including the fees and costs of experts, together with reasonable attorney's fees; and

ix. Grant such other and further relief as the Court shall deem just, proper and equitable.

Dated: New York, New York
March 8, 2000
LAW OFFICE OF JOSEPH P. GARLAND
By: Joseph P. Garland—JG0888
217 Broadway, Suite 404
New York, NY 10007
(212) 213-1812
(212) 213-1816 (fax)
LAW OFFICES OF MEL URBACH
By: Mel Urbach
One Exchange Place
Suite 1000
Jersey City, NJ 07302
(201) 395-4709
(201) 395-4711 (fax)
KLEIN & SOLOMON, LLP
By: Edward E. Klein
Jay Solomon
275 Madison Avenue
11th Floor
New York, NY 10016
(212) 661-9400
(212) 661-6606 (fax)
MILLER FAUCHER AND CAFFERTY LLP
By: Marvin A. Miller (MM 9210)
Adam J. Levitt
30 North La Salle Street
Suite 3200
Chicago, IL 60602
(312) 782-4880

(312) 782-4485 (fax)
MILLER FAUCHER AND CAFFERTY LLP
By: J. Dennis Faucher
Michael C. Dell'Angelo
One Penn Square West
30 S. 15th Street
Philadelphia, PA 19102
(215) 864-2800
(215) 864-2810 (fax)
BERGER & MONTAGUE, P.C.
By: Stephen A. Whinston
Edward W. Millstein
1622 Locust Street
Philadelphia, PA 19103-6365
(215) 875-3000
(215) 875-3053 (fax)
AZULAY & AZULAY, P.C.
By: J. Daniel Azulay
One East Wacker Drive, Suite 2700
Chicago, IL 60601-2001
(312) 832-9200
(312) 832-9212 (fax)
GOODKIND   LABATON   RUDOFF   &
SUCHAROW
By: Kenneth F. McCallion
Rajan Sharma
100 Park Avenue
New York, NY 10017
(212) 907-0700
(212) 818-0477 (fax)
LAW OFFICE OF KENNETH A. ELAN
By: Kenneth A. Elan
217 Broadway, Suite 404
New York, NY 10007
(212) 619-0261

(212) 385-2707 (fax)
Attorneys for Plaintiff
To: WHITE & CASE
             Owen Pell
             1155 Sixth Avenue
             New York, NY 10036
             (212) 819-8891
             Attorneys for Defendants